THE EFFECTIVE INTERPRETING SERIES

Cognitive Processing Skills in English

Carol J. Patrie

The Effective Interpreter Series: Cognitive Processing Skills in English

Producer: Joe Dannis

Manufactured in the United States of America.

Published by DawnSignPress.

Cover Design: Greg Smith

ISBN: 978-1-58121-166-5

10 9 8 7 6 5 4 3

The Rosetta Stone

The Rosetta Stone appears throughout the series as a symbol of translation's importance to mankind. The basalt slab was discovered in July 1799 in the small Egyptian village of Rosette on the western delta of the Nile. The stone's inscription in hieroglyphic, demotic, and Greek languages led to a crucial breakthrough in research regarding Egyptian hieroglyphs. This key to "translating silent images" into a living language symbolizes the importance of accurate transmissions of messages from one language into another.

The Rosetta Stone now resides in the British Museum in London.

Contents

Acknowledgments

A work like this takes the dedicated involvement of many people. Each of these people has shaped my overall vision for this work and the series of which it is a part. The vision I hold is that this work will assist interpreters, interpreters in training, and their teachers as they improve their skills in interpretation and, in so doing will enhance the field of interpretation as a whole. Joe Dannis is the *sine qua non* of this work. Without Joe's steady encouragement and support this work would never have reached fruition. Joe unwaveringly has believed in me and my vision from the very start. Such unconditional support is most rare and deeply appreciated. I thank Yoon Lee and Phil Carmona for their persistent attention to detail in the seemingly endless task of video editing. I am grateful to Earl Fleetwood for his valuable feedback on the content of this book and for his suggestions for improvement. Bob Johnson offered assistance during the development of some of the ideas in this book and in their organization. I thank Joseph Josselyn for his superb video editing skills, enthusiasm, and dedication to the project. I deeply appreciate Melanie Metzger's insightful review of the manuscript and video. From the beginning, Becky Ryan shared her wonderful literary gifts and talents with me. Her analysis and feedback made this work better than I imagined it could be. I often thought I could not work to her standard, but did anyway and surprised myself. She has been a steady source of encouragement and strength in all phases of this project. Special gratitude goes to her for the "timely reminders" and for sharing her perspective on the things that really matter.

Dedication

This work is dedicated to my parents, Stanley and Jean Patrie. They have always believed in my work and in me. Now they each can view my work from their respective realms.

Preface

When I became a professional interpreter in 1968, interpreter education for sign language interpreters was a rare thing. Since that time, interpreter education has made great strides. I am pleased to share with you my years of experience as an interpreter and years of experience as an interpreter educator. I am one of the developers of the Master of Arts in Interpretation at Gallaudet University, where I taught interpretation. The ideas and exercises presented in this book are the result of my work developing materials that practicing and future interpreters can use in or out of the classroom while they study interpretation.

In my experience I have found that one of the greatest problems in interpreter education is a lack of materials for use in the classroom. An even more severe problem is the lack of study materials that practicing and future interpreters can use on their own, either for refresher practice or for continuing professional development. Interpretation is a very complex skill that requires hours and hours of appropriate practice. Often interpreters cannot find effective ways to improve their skills. It is my hope that by providing these materials for developing and improving cognitive processing skills, practicing and future interpreters will find rewarding and effective outcomes.

Successful interpreters rely on many skills in their everyday work. The development of these skills is not intuitive or automatic. Most of the skills needed during the interpretation process must be developed through a careful sequence of learning activities. The learning process for interpretation should begin with strengthening skills in your first language (L1), in this case, English. These materials provide an innovative and exciting way to develop the cognitive processing skills in English that will develop into strong interpreting skills.

This book provides specific approaches and guidelines for teaching cognitive processing skills in English. The units in the accompanying student DVD and workbook are sequenced so that less challenging units are presented first, followed by more challenging units. The units are Comprehension, Memory, Acuity and Discrimination, Immediate Repetition, Delayed Repetition, Number Repetition, Word-Level Pattern Inference (formerly called cloze), Phrase-Level Pattern Inference, (formerly called prediction), and Multitasking. This sequenced approach leads to greater reliability in developing interpreting skills.

Description of the Materials

Each set of materials includes a workbook, and a videotext. In the upper right corner of the videotext you will see the unit and exercise number. For example Ex. 1.2 means the second exercise in Unit 1.

Introduction to Cognitive Processing Skills in English

What Are Cognitive Processing Skills?

Cognitive Processing is the term I use to describe some of the invisible mental processes that are essential to the interpreting process. These mental processes include comprehension, memory, acuity and discrimination, immediate repetition, number repetition, delayed repetition, word-level pattern inference, phrase-level pattern inference and multitasking. Each of these terms is explained in the workbook along with exercises to allow you to practice each skill. It is essential to have these basic processing mechanisms under control before learning and developing other skills in the interpretation process. The interpreter needs to be able to process linguistically complex material as quickly and efficiently as possible. Gonzalez et al. (1991) point out that the routinization of complex tasks, such as those listed here, can reduce the amount of conscious effort needed for the interpretation process. These authors go on to say that the complicated skills in the interpretation process can be positively affected by training. Once these complex tasks become more routinized, then the interpreter's attention can be channeled to deal with more consciously demanding tasks such as register and stylistic issues. These authors remind us that multiple tasks must occur simultaneously during the interpretation process.

There are other important cognitive processes involved in the interpreting process, such as linguistic processing in at least two languages, processing of situational, contextual, and cultural information. A separate volume in this series deals with improving skills in English.

Why Develop Cognitive Processing Skills?

Successful interpreters have many skills that they rely on in their everyday work. Quick access to cognitive processing skills underlies many of the more complicated aspects of the interpretation process. This means that interpreters must be able to quickly make sense out of what they see and hear, decide what the message means and how to transfer that message into another language with split-second accuracy. Shreve and Koby (1997) point out that during the last 25 years, there has been much interest in trying to describe the cognitive processes associated with interpreting. They point out that these mental operations are largely "hidden" yet, form a complex and essential part of the interpretation process.

The process of mastering cognitive processing skills is best begun in one's first language (L1). The importance of developing and refining skills in L1 is often overlooked in interpreter education. Some may think that being able to read, speak, and understand in one's L1 is enough, and that it is only necessary to study a second language (L2), while neglecting development of L1 skills. This is not the case. Roberts (1992) supports the idea of competency in two languages. She says, "Language competency, which covers the ability to manipulate with ease and accuracy the two languages involved in the interpreting process, is a prerequisite for successful interpreting of a message, for the message is mediated through language" (p.1). She further subdivides the idea of language competency by saying language competency includes the "ability to understand the source language in all its nuances and the ability to express oneself correctly, fluently, clearly and with poise in the target language" (p. 2).

An effective interpretation will rely just as heavily on good skills in L1 as on the skills in the interpreter's L2. Interpreter education programs must place an increased focus on developing high levels of linguistic ability in interpretation students' L1s. Moreover, cognitive processing skills must be well developed in both languages. When cognitive skills are well developed, less effort is needed to process information. Because simultaneous interpreting is a very difficult task, it is best to reduce the effort needed by mastering the component skills before combining them into the more cognitively complex simultaneous interpretation.

The simultaneous interpretation process is not actually a linear sequence of skills that are performed one at a time. Actually, the various parts of the process, listening, analyzing, transferring the message into another language, and finding expression for that idea, all interact with each other as the speaker continues speaking and the interpreter continues interpreting. It can be overwhelming and not very successful to try to master all the parts of the process of simultaneous interpretation at once. Instead, it is better to learn how to master the component skills in the interpretation process and then synthesize the component skills into the process of simultaneous interpretation. Hopefully, the feeling of mastery of the components of the interpretation process will lead to successful synthesis of these components, and this synthesis will in turn lead to job satisfaction when the new interpreter enters the field. If a new interpreter is well prepared to enter the job market, then it is more likely that this interpreter will demonstrate high levels of professionalism.

Higher levels of professionalism can lead to greater consumer satisfaction and greater recognition of the profession of interpretation overall. The exercises in this book and DVD have been developed with the goal of increasing cognitive processing capacities.

The systematic development of the cognitive processing skills that underlie the interpretation process is very important. If these skills are not developed and available, then there is a much higher chance that the skills that must be developed later, such as translation, consecutive interpretation, and simultaneous interpretation will not be strongly grounded and may be more difficult to master. A deficit in cognitive processing skills could result in interpretations that are skewed or that contain an error. Specific cognitive processing skill deficits can lead to particular types of errors in interpretation. For example, we may find that there is a relationship between poor auditory memory, short lag time, and an increase in overall errors (Cokely, 1992a). The development of cognitive processing skills can reduce the amount of effortful processing that is required to perform a successful simultaneous interpretation.

Reliable cognitive processing skills are of utmost importance to practicing and future interpreters. Gile (1997) points out that even the performance of practicing interpreters who enjoy excellent professional reputations can contain errors such as wrong numbers, wrong names, or wrong propositional content and that these errors can occur up to several times per minute. He goes on to explain that these errors can occur even under the best working conditions. The interpreters he refers to do not have apparent "weaknesses in terms of the source language or target language proficiency, world knowledge or interpreting skills" (p. 197). Gile suggests there is an intrinsic difficulty in interpreting and that the difficulty lies in the cognitive processing tasks involved.

To provide a framework for his ideas, Gile developed the Effort Model. In this model, Gile provides a powerful explanation for the importance of cognitive processing capacity in the interpretation process. He also points out that this processing capacity is available in limited supply and is not automatic. Gile divides his model into three parts, the Listen and Analyze Effort, which deals with comprehension, the Production Effort, which includes speech planning and verbal output, and the Memory Effort, which deals with the stresses placed on the short-term memory system. These materials provide a clear approach to developing the cognitive processing skills that make up the components of the Effort Model. An emphasis is placed on analyzing the development of cognitive processing skills by providing exercises, study questions, and a way to examine those answers in a follow-up process that gives insight into strategies for further developing cognitive processing skills.

The Goal of This Workbook and Video

The purpose of the workbook and accompanying DVD is to improve and enhance your skills in English so that you will have a strong understanding of English usage before you attempt to interpret from or to English. It is important to develop English skills with conscious effort, even if English is your first language. You may not have had the opportunity before now to study your first language as an adult. If English is your second language, this workbook provides you with specific skills that will build confidence in your English skills. As you use this workbook your English skills improve and your awareness of the importance of these skills improves.

An increased awareness of English usage leads to a more reliable interpretation. A reliable interpretation naturally communicates as much as possible of the original meaning. So, it is important to be sure that the meaning of the original message has been correctly analyzed and understood, as far as conditions permit. The seven units in this workbook are designed to provide practice in intralingual skills in English to help ensure that the original message is correctly understood and analyzed. Strong intralingual skills in English are a stepping stone to professional-level simultaneous interpretation skills.

The simultaneous interpretation process is not actually a linear sequence of skills performed one at a time. The various parts of the simultaneous interpretation process, listening, analyzing, transferring the message into another language, and finding expression for that idea, all interact with each other as the speaker continues speaking and the interpreter continues interpreting. It can be overwhelming and not very successful to try to master all the parts of the process at once. Instead, it is more effective to learn how to master the component skills in the interpretation process and then synthesize the component skills into the process of simultaneous interpretation.

Just as the overall process of interpretation is not really linear, the component skills are not linear either. During the actual process of interpretation, specific English skills are dynamic and interact with each other and with other processes. English skills do not appear as discrete units in the interpretation process. Seven important English skills are presented in this workbook. These English skills are separated into seven units in this workbook for two reasons. First, ineffective results commonly are achieved when a student attempts to learn the interpretation process as a whole and has no prior experience in interpretation. The second reason for separating the seven skills is the easy identification of a problem area. Separating the component skills allows you to experience mastery of the components of the larger process.

Models of the Interpretation Process

There are a number of models of the interpretation process. No two are exactly alike, but all models suggest that interpretation is a multistage process. Moser (1997) summarizes some of the better known models of interpretation. She mentions the following models: Gerver (1976), Moser-Mercer (1978), Kitano (1993), Pradis (1994), and a summary of Daro and Fabbro's (1994) model of memory during interpretation. Moser points out that many models use an information processing approach to explain the interpretation process. Information systems models are based on computer-style operations. This kind of analysis will be necessarily somewhat flawed since human minds do not operate exactly as do computers. Another point that Moser makes is that even though most researchers will agree that interpretation is a multistage process, they do not agree on the names of the stages or the contents of the stages. Moser states that "A powerful model of the interpreting process must be broad enough to include aspects that reflect the complex, time constrained multitasking environment of simultaneous interpreting that involves a high degree of cognitive processing" (1997, p. 194). For detailed information on the models mentioned, please refer to the chapter by Moser in Danks (1997).

In this workbook, I emphasize Gile's (1995) Effort Model because it provides a clear and simple framework for the importance of cognitive processing tasks. Gile's Effort Model provides a powerful explanation for the importance of developing intralingual skills before learning the interpretation process. The model shows that processing capacity for interpreting is available in limited supply and is not automatic.

According to Gile (1995), many of the mental operations required in the interpretation process are nonautomatic and require conscious effort. He suggests that there are three main effort areas in the interpretation process. The first is the Listen and Analysis Effort, which deals with comprehension, the Production Effort, which includes speech planning and verbal output, and the Memory Effort, which deals with the stresses placed on the short-term memory system. These three efforts are integrated by the Coordination Effort. Gile also suggests that each interpreter has certain capacities within each of these areas of effort. Ideally, the interpreter has more capacity than is currently required by the interpretation task. This workbook provides clear approaches to developing the intralingual skills that make up the components of the Effort Model.

Regardless of which model of interpretation you choose to study, you will soon see that all models require that the incoming message be analyzed and understood before any part of the transfer process can begin. In order to accomplish an accurate analysis of the incoming English message, it is essential to have strong English intralingual skills.

When to Learn Cognitive Processing Skills?

If you are a novice, or new interpreter, cognitive processing skills should be developed before moving on to more advanced skills, which compose the interpretation process. If you are beyond the beginning stages of an interpreter education program, or are already an experienced interpreter, you can also benefit from practice in cognitive processing skills, either as a refresher course or for professional skill maintenance.

Students in interpreter education programs may experience the plateau effect in training. The plateau effect is that point when skills appear to be no longer developing as rapidly as they did earlier in the training process. This is a common occurrence. When progress seems to be stagnating, it is often useful to go back to an earlier stage of skill development and practice at that earlier level. Taking time to go back and review skills is a positive step because it increases confidence, builds mastery, and often provides the springboard to further progress.

Experienced interpreters who are now working may not have had the benefit of studying the individual skills that make up the interpretation process. Experienced interpreters often search for specific ways to improve their interpretation skills. Practice on the components of the interpretation process, such as cognitive processing skills, can be meaningful and productive practice for the experienced interpreter who wishes to work independently on skill improvement. Strong and quick cognitive processing skills form a good basis on which to develop or practice more complex skills in the interpretation process.

Specific Cognitive Processing Skills

In the past, the following terms have been used to refer to the cognitive processing skills that form part of the interpretation process: shadowing, prediction, and cloze. These terms have been borrowed from cognitive psychology and in their truest definitions are somewhat misleading as they relate to the interpretation process. In this workbook, terms that are as transparent and as accurate as possible will be used in order to promote a clear understanding of the processes involved.

The term *prediction* has been widely used in the interpreter education field to encompass the process of completing sentences or ideas. In actuality, the term means to make known in advance on the basis of special knowledge; to foretell or prophesy. These words contain connotations that contradict many of the central tenets of the interpretation process. Interpreters may reasonably be expected to infer what information would logically fit in the given context, but not simply to guess or imagine without a reasoned basis. The term cloze has been borrowed from the field of language acquisition and was originally intended as a measure of language proficiency in reading. Both prediction and cloze are actually pattern inference exercises, thus, the broader, more accurate term of *pattern inference* is used in this workbook.

Here are the basic terms and their meanings as they are used in this workbook:

Comprehension

The American Heritage Dictionary defines comprehension as taking in the meaning or importance of something. To grasp. Dancette (1997) says "To understand a text is to build a meaningful and coherent representation of its conceptual content" (p. 78).

Memory

The American Heritage Dictionary defines memory as the mental capacity of recalling or recognizing previously learned behavior or past experience.

Acuity and Discrimination

Acuity means acuteness or sharpness of perception; keen perception. Discrimination means the ability to perceive distinguishing features, to distinguish, or to recognize as distinct.

Immediate Repetition

Immediate repetition means to say or perform again without delay. This type of repetition is begun as soon as the listener can begin processing what he or she has heard. There is no enforced delay in this kind of repetition. This term replaces the older term shadowing.

Delayed Repetition

Delayed repetition means to say or perform again with a delay. This type of repetition is characterized by an enforced delay before the repetition process begins. The delay could be either a short time interval or an idea unit. This term replaces the older term of shadowing with delay.

Shadowing

Has been widely used in interpreter education to mean repetition and has been subdivided into phonemic shadowing and phrase shadowing. The dictionary indicates that shadowing means to cast a dark cloud or to represent vaguely, mysteriously or prophetically, or to change by gradual degrees. These terms do not reveal the intent of this cognitive skill clearly. So, in this text, *immediate repetition* and *delayed repetition* are used, rather than phonemic shadowing and phrase shadowing.

Number Repetition

This term is used to describe the process of repeating speeches that contain numbers. Repetition with numbers can be done with or without delay.

Pattern Inference

A pattern is defined as a model or original used as an archetype or a model to be followed in making things. Inference means the act of deriving logical conclusions from information known to be true, or, reasoning from factual knowledge or evidence. Here, two types of pattern inference exercises are presented, word-level pattern inference and phrase-level pattern inference.

Word-Level Pattern Inference

Word-level pattern inference means to infer a single word that can logically fit in the context provided. This term replaces the term *cloze*.

Phrase-Level Pattern Inference

Phrase-level pattern inference means to infer a phrase that can logically fit in the context provided. This term replaces the older term *prediction*.

Multitasking

Multitasking means to perform a series of specific tasks at the same time for the purpose of cognitive processing development as it relates to the simultaneous interpretation process. An example is performing immediate repetition while performing a distracter task such as writing numbers.

Process and Product

In interpreter education there is always much discussion over whether students should focus on the process of interpretation or the product of the interpretation. My position is that both are equally important and should be part of even the earliest stages of training. It is vital that you understand the difference between these two terms and the role they play in your education and training as an interpreter. The process of interpretation is largely invisible. The process is what goes on in your head as you listen, analyze, transfer the meaning to another language, and find expression for that message in another language. This part of the interpretation event cannot be recorded or observed by another person. Only via introspection can interpreters gain insight into their own process and make changes to it. Gile (1995) suggests that adopting a process-oriented approach can optimize training time. In his opinion it is best not to focus only on the end products of the translation process, but rather to include information on "principles, methods and procedures" (p.10). Gile goes on to support his idea this way: "By concentrating on the *reasons* for errors or good choices in Translation rather than on the words or structures produced by the students, teachers devote most of their effective teaching time to Translation *strategies* and lose little time over their by-products" (p.11).

On the other hand the product is the observable part of your work. It is the interpretation that the "listener" receives from the "sender" via your interpretation. The product can be recorded for future analysis, while the process cannot. Seal has summarized the results of a recent study of interpreters who wished to improve their skills. In that report, she emphasizes the importance of analyzing one's own work. "Self-analysis, the zenith of any professional development activity, is highly facilitated when we step back and take a look at ourselves. Routine videotaping and observing videotaped performances for strengths and weaknesses and for changes over time is quite possibly the most valuable, yet least frequently accomplished activity we can engage in" (Seal, 1999 p. 14).

This workbook is designed to assist in the development of specific cognitive *processes* in the interpretation process. The development of these processes is accomplished through a combination of strategies. The first step is to read the information in the chapter, which provides you with insight into the importance of the process and the product. Next, you actually perform the exercise and record your work. This gives you an opportunity to experience the process and also to create a *product.* In the next step, you answer the study questions. The answers to the study questions allow you to focus on product in order to see if your work is accurate or needs improvement. In the follow-up process, your focus shifts back to the process of interpretation. By examining your product, and redoing the exercises and studying how the product varies from one try to the next, you gain a deeper insight into how variations on the process that are under your control can affect the product.

How to Use This Book

The cognitive processing skills in this text are comprehension, memory, acuity and discrimination, immediate repetition, delayed repetition, number repetition, word-level pattern inference, phrase-level pattern inference, and multitasking. Exercises are provided for each of these units. All of the exercises in each unit may be completed as out-of-classroom work. Some of the exercises may also be done in a group format. The exercises in Unit 1. Comprehension; Unit 2. Memory; Unit 3. Acuity and Discrimination, and the additional exercises for these units can be used in a group format or classroom setting.

For either independent or group work, this workbook provides complete directions for each exercise. For the exercises with spoken English material, the directions guide you to the correct location on the accompanying DVD. The accompanying DVD is closed-captioned, however you should rely on the spoken word rather than the captions in order to develop the necessary cognitive skills. Each video selection is transcribed in your book and each line in the transcript is numbered to make class discussion easier. Each exercise has study questions and a follow-up process. The study questions provide focus and insight into your responses to the exercises. The follow-up process after each exercise is a form of self-assessment. The workbook exercises and follow-up process provide the opportunity to take responsibility for not only creating work, but for developing strategies for improvement. At the end of each unit there is a progress-tracking sheet. Use this sheet to note the date you completed the exercises and to make notes regarding your progress and also to record any questions you may have about the exercise.

What You Will Need before Beginning the Exercises

You will need specific equipment in order to get the maximum benefit from these exercises. Here is what you will need: a DVD player with a remote control that will allow pausing and frame advance, a TV monitor, an audio recorder, a blank audio tape, a quiet place to work, a copy of the DVD that accompanies this workbook, and this workbook. Owning a video camera would enhance the study process and is optional.

When and Where You Should Plan to Do the Exercises

Each exercise can be done independently. This means that you should either plan to do them out of class on your own time or in a class format if your training program has a place for you to record your work. Where you do the exercises will depend on your instructor and the equipment available in your interpreter education program. For example if your program has a language lab that will permit you to work independently and to record your work, then you can do many of the exercises independently while on campus. Exercises in Units 1, 2, and 3 may be done in a group setting without individual recording devices for each student. Your teacher may introduce the exercises to you and go over your results with you. Your teacher may also provide similar exercises for you to work on in class, or you may work on some of these exercises in class, depending on your teacher's instructions and lesson plans.

If you are a practicing interpreter and want to work on developing your skills you will still need all of the equipment listed above and may proceed at your own pace. You may wish to form a study group with other interpreters in order to have a forum in which to discuss your skill-development work.

How Many Times Should You Do the Exercises?

You can benefit from doing each exercise at least twice. This process is called redoing your work. When you do the exercise the first time, the material that you listen to will be "cold" or unfamiliar. The cognitive processes that you are practicing may be new and unfamiliar as well. When you do the exercise the second time, the material will be "warm," or familiar, because you have heard it once before. You will also be more comfortable with the process the second time. It is a good idea to practice the exercises more than once because this type of practice will allow you to experience good control of the process that you are working on.

The Five-Step Follow-up

The five-step follow-up is presented after each exercise.

The five parts of the follow-up are

Step 1 **Observation**

Step 2 **Selection**

Step 3 **Analysis**

Step 4 **Assessment**

Step 5 **Action**

The purpose of the follow-up process is to introduce and strengthen the concepts of self-assessment and insight into the process of interpretation. Interpreters who have accurate self-assessment skills can enjoy lifelong learning and continuing education opportunities in a wide variety of settings, even if a teacher or mentor is not available. Self-assessment skills lead to accountability in interpretation because they allow you to analyze both the process and product of your work. Accountability in interpretation means that interpreters can make conscious decisions about both the products and processes involved in their interpretations and work to see that the interpretations are faithful to the original message. It also means that the interpreter can take responsibility when the interpretation is not faithful to the message and correct the interpretation. A graduate of the Master of Arts in Interpretation at Gallaudet who became very familiar with this process suggests that the impact of the self-assessment available through the follow-up process is unparalleled. (Fleetwood, 1998, personal communication).

In addition to increasing accountability in interpretation, the follow-up process of self-assessment allows an objective analysis of either the product or the processes involved in interpretation. In this workbook, which deals specifically with the development of cognitive processing skills, the emphasis is placed on gaining insight into the processes involved in arriving at the production of the component parts of the interpretation. In later components of this series of workbooks, the emphasis of the follow-up will be placed on the final product of the interpretation. This five-step approach to analysis allows for commentary on the work performed rather than on the interpreter who performed it.

By carefully doing each follow-up, you will learn the importance of the many components of the interpretation process and that each, performed well, is needed for a successful interpretation. By being able to separate the process into its component parts and processes, you can better understand where to focus your efforts for improvement. Naturally, the interpretation process is not a segmented event in real life, and one should study it in manageable pieces at first. This kind of follow-up allows you to determine which parts of your work are successful attempts and which parts are less successful. More importantly, it helps you to see which parts of the interpretation process are under your control and which are not.

The five-step follow-up is an exciting new way to improve your awareness of your performance. All students want to know "How am I doing so far?" By putting forth the effort to work through the follow-up process, many students will be able to answer this question for themselves instead of relying on a teacher to provide feedback. You can think of it as a mystery. What was missing? What was good? What accounts for my success in the exercises? Why did I miss some aspects? The sooner you can adopt an analytical view of your own work, the sooner your progress in interpretation skills can become reliable. You will also feel less lost in the details of learning the very complex skill of interpretation. You will feel a certain mastery and sense of accomplishment and control over your own progress.

The follow-up should be completed as soon as possible after completing the exercises. This is important as you may be asked to explain why you chose certain answers. You will better be able to explain your thinking if you do the follow-up immediately after the exercises. If you are working in a group, the questions and activities in the follow-up could be used in a group discussion format. If you are working in a group format, it is still important to write your answers so you can refer to them later and see how much progress you have made in the area of self-assessment.

A more complete explanation of the follow-up is given on pages 19–23.

Progress Tracking Sheet

Use this sheet to track your progress with the exercises you have completed. After performing the exercise, answering the study questions, and doing the follow-up, fill in the tracking sheet. Note the date that you completed the exercise and give an indication of your level of accomplishment. You can use either a quantitative or qualitative approach to track your progress.

A quantitative approach uses a point scale. Assigning points to linguistic exercises is arbitrary, but in academic environments you may find the point system more suitable than the qualitative approach. Here is an example of a scale you can use to assign points to your work. Excellent (no serious errors) = 5 points, Good (some errors, but not serious) = 4 points, Fair (many errors, some serious) = 3 points, Not satisfactory = 2 (many errors, most are serious), Poor = 1 point. (Missed the point of the exercise—must redo).

Each performance, each study question, and each follow-up step can be assigned a point value. A zero indicates that the question was not answered and a 5 indicates a full and complete answer. Add the scores in each column (not row) and divide by the number of exercises to get a percentage for first performance, second performance, study questions, and follow-up. It is important to have separate percentages for each of these columns because the scores represent different skills. Remember that a second performance on the same material is considered practice on "warm" or familiar material and should be weighted less than the "cold" or first performance.

A qualitative approach is well suited to those who are studying the material in an independent fashion or those who do not want to attach numbers and percentages to their work. In a qualitative approach you describe your response to your work rather than assigning numbers. Write down enough information to remind yourself of your level of achievement in the performance of the exercises, study questions and follow-up.

The sample chart provides examples of how to note your progress using the quantitative or qualitative approach.

Exercise Number	Date	First Performance	Study Questions	Follow-up Activity	Questions and Reminders	Date	Second Performance
Exercise 1 Quantitative	10/3	50/50 = 100%	20/25 = 80%	20/25 = 80%		11/5	
Qualitative		I understood the passage.	I thought I understood all the vocabulary but missed two words.	This is a new process for me. Not sure of my answers.	I need to concentrate while listening.		Did not do over. Wanted to move to second exercise.
Exercise 2 Quantitative	10/9	40/50 = 80%	20/25 = 80%	20/25 = 80%		11/15	50/50 = 100%
Qualitative		I did not feel that I understood everything he said.	This passage is harder than the first. I did a complete job of answering the questions but not use of all.	I have more confidence in my analysis work.	Look up the word that referred to a disease in fish. Concentrate.		I concentrated and felt that I comprehended better.
Exercise 3 Quantitative	10/15	30/50 = 60%	15/25 = 60%	20/25 = 80%		11/21	40/50 = 80%
Qualitative		I got lost in listening and did not concentrate.	Was not able to answer the questions because my concentration was low.	This helped me to analyze my listening. This helped.	Attend to details. Concentrate		Much better the second time. Listened for details and concentrated.
Quantitative Totals		80%	73%	80%			90%

UNIT 1

Comprehension of Source Material

Introduction

Interpreters must understand the source material before they can begin the interpretation process. Comprehension of the source material is a skill that underlies all other skills in cognitive processing skill development as well as in the interpretation process as a whole.

According to Gile (1995), comprehension is based on two basic features. One is knowledge of words in a language and the other is knowledge of the grammar of a language. He also says that these two basic features are not enough to ensure comprehension. The context in which the words and grammar are used is an essential ingredient in the comprehension process.

The comprehension process generally begins with a message in the source language (SL). When this message is sent to a receiver and understood by that receiver, basic communication is thought to have occurred. In reality, this is much too simple, because as Gile points out, each receiver or listener's prior knowledge, knowledge of the vocabulary, the grammar and context will influence their understanding. In general the more information, or extralinguistic knowledge, a person has, the more likely they are to understand the message as intended by the sender. Naturally, the process of communication via an interpreter is much more complicated than when two people who share the same language are speaking to each other. In the case of an interpreted message several more steps must occur. The message in the SL is sent to and received by the interpreter. The interpreter must understand the meaning of the SL message and then translate the message and give that message expression in another language, called the target language (TL). The person who receives the interpreted message ideally will understand the message as intended by the original sender of the message.

The Role of Comprehension in the Interpretation Process

Gonzalez et al. (1991) provide a good summary of the role of comprehension in the interpretation process. They suggest that there are three basic parts to this process. The first is that the interpreter is a *receptor* who hears the message and analyzes it for meaning. The interpreter's prior knowledge and familiarity with the language help the interpreter to reject any irrelevant or nonsensical meanings. The second is that the interpreter breaks up the message into workable chunks in a process called *segmentation* (Kelly, 1979). This process allows the interpreter to focus on meaning units regardless of how many words are in the message. In this part of the process, the interpreter sets aside the form and discovers the meaning of the message. In the third step, the interpreter formulates a version of the message in the TL, or the language into which the message is to be interpreted.

Gile (1995) devotes an entire chapter to the importance of comprehension in the interpretation process in his book entitled *Basic Concepts and Models for Interpreter and Translator Training*. One of the points he stresses is that the interpreter's need for extralinguistic knowledge (ELK) never levels off, but rather, increases. Next, he stresses the importance of "deliberate and sustained analysis" (p. 85). This can be likened to an ongoing process of checking probable meanings with the current context to see if these make sense and if these probable meanings are likely to be the meanings intended by the speaker. Another important point from Gile is that the type of understanding or comprehension that the interpreter must use is not the same as that used by a layperson. The difference is the intensity with which the interpreter must constantly listen and analyze the incoming message.

The comprehension exercises are arranged from easiest to most difficult. Before beginning these, refer back to page 9 and go over the list of things you will need before beginning the exercises. While you are working keep in mind that you are now listening in a focused and intense way so that you can analyze the incoming message. Think of Gile's idea of deliberate and sustained analysis as you listen carefully to each selection.

Comprehension Exercises

EXERCISE 1.1

Introduction

JEFF HARDISON

Directions

It will take approximately one minute to listen to the selection. After listening fill in the answers to the study questions. Then do the follow-up. Find a quiet place to work where you will not be interrupted while working on this exercise. Find this selection on your DVD. Adjust the volume as necessary. Be sure you can see the screen clearly. Begin by allowing yourself time to focus on the speaker's face. Listen to Jeff Hardison's short introduction. Do not write while listening. You do not need to record your answers on video or audiotape. After watching this selection, answer the study questions in the space provided.

Study Questions

1. Use a dictionary to look up any new words. Find synonyms for as many words as you can.

____

____

____

____

____

____

____

2. What is the speaker's purpose in this selection?

3. Why does the name Hardison belie the fact that he grew up in a Cuban family?

4. The speaker says he grew up in a Cuban family with that language and culture. What are the possible meanings of this sentence? Does he say his family is Cuban? What language did he grow up with? What culture did he grow up with? What do you know of that culture? Look up Cuban culture and list some of the characteristics of that culture.

5. List other features of the talk that you would like to look up. For example, where is Cuba located? Where is the University of Florida located?

Transcript for *Introduction,* Jeff Hardison

Hello, my name is Jeff Hardison. Although that last name belies the fact that I grew up in a Cuban family with both that language and culture. Um, I originally grew up in Florida and have moved to Washington, DC. Actually, I just moved to Virginia, which is where I am currently living. Uh, I have a BA from the University of Florida in English. I have a Masters degree from Gallaudet University in Linguistics and I currently work at Gallaudet University as a staff interpreter.

Sample Follow-up—Pat's Answers

The five-step follow-up is explained below. The answers of a hypothetical student named Pat are shown here and discussed in order to help you get started on your own five-step follow-up.

Here are sample answers to each part of the follow-up.

Step 1 Observation

Review your answers.

Begin by taking a close look at your answers to the exercises. When you examine your own work to see where your strengths and weaknesses lie, you gain several immediate benefits. The first is that you will gain self-confidence because you will know exactly where you stand in relation to being able to perform the cognitive processing tasks and how these tasks relate to the overall process of simultaneous interpretation. Second, you will know exactly which cognitive skills need further attention from you. Many future interpreters feel overwhelmed by the enormity of the process of learning simultaneous interpretation. Using objective observation skills on your answers to each question can reduce the feeling of being overwhelmed and somewhat "lost" in the details of learning the process of interpretation.

Your answers will either be written in this book or recorded on tape for you to review. In either case, this will allow you to take an objective look at how you performed. For example when Pat has completed comprehension exercise 1, s/he will refer to the answers to the study questions. Here is a sample of Pat's work. Pat's answers are in italics.

1. Use a dictionary to look up any new words. Find synonyms for as many words as you can.

   Belies—disguises or misrepresents

   BA—stands for Bachelor of Arts degree. This is a four-year undergraduate degree in the United States.

   Find synonyms for:

   Last name: family name, surname

   Grew up: matured, reached maturity

   Washington, DC: Nation's capital, Capital of the United States, District of Columbia

   Just (moved): recently relocated

   Currently: presently, now

2. What is the speaker's purpose in this selection?

   His purpose is to provide a quick introduction of himself to the video audience. Note his level of education and his current position. He has a Master's degree and is a professional full-time interpreter on the Gallaudet University campus.

3. Why does the name Hardison belie the fact that he grew up in a Cuban family?

   Hardison does not sound like a Hispanic name. It sounds more like a British name.

4. The speaker says he grew up in a Cuban family with that language and culture. What are the possible meanings of this sentence? Does he say his family is Cuban? What language did he grow up with? What culture did he grow up with? What do you know of that culture? Look up Cuban culture and list some of the characteristics of that culture.

   Cuban families often speak Spanish and may embrace Hispanic culture, even though they do not currently live in Cuba.

   He does not say his family is Cuban. It is implied. However, it cannot be assumed.

   Ask students to check the World Wide Web or the library to find information on Cuba and Hispanic culture. He implies that he grew up in a home where Hispanic culture was valued and promoted.

   If you have Hispanic students in your class, invite them to tell about their experiences in Spanish-speaking homes or cultures.

5. List other features of the introduction that you would like to look up. For example, where is Cuba located? Where is the University of Florida located?

   Interpretation students' geography skills may be weak. Provide a wall map of the world. Have students locate Cuba and note the names of the bodies of water near it. On a map of Florida locate the University of Florida. Does it have more than one campus?

Step 2 **Selection**

Select the portions of work that are most satisfactory and select the portions that need further attention.

In this step, you will decide which answers are appropriate for the situation. In many cases, there will be more than one acceptable answer or solution. In interpretation, it is not likely that there will be only one "right" answer because there are many variables in language usage. You will also select the portions of your answers that you are not sure about or that you are sure are not acceptable.

In the sample of Pat's work we see that some questions are not fully answered. Pat should select the answers to questions 1, 3, 4, and 5 and take time to find the answers. This can be done in group study or by checking in an encyclopedia or on the World Wide Web. In this further effort, Pat learns that "belie" could be replaced with "disguises." Pat has learned that Hardison is not a typically Hispanic name, it sounds more English than Hispanic and that information on Cuba, its location, language and culture can be found on the Web or in an encyclopedia.

Step 3 **Analysis**

Analyze for accuracy.

In this step you examine your answers and see if you answered the questions posed. You will do this by listening to the exercise again and reading the accompanying transcript. Each transcript has line numbers to help you keep track of your place. In doing this you will see exactly what was said in the original speech. This part of the process will allow you to see exactly where your successes and errors are located within the exercise text.

By the time Pat has arrived at this step, Pat should have completed the answers to the study questions by spending more time and effort to find the complete answers to the questions. It is important to be able to answer the comprehension questions or the speech will not be fully understood.

Step 4 **Assessment**

Look for underlying reasons for successes or errors.

This part of the process allows you to ask "Why?" Why was that a good solution or why was that solution not acceptable? For example, you might realize that you misheard what was said or you misunderstood what was said. This part of the process is very important and you should not allow yourself to say, "I don't know why I said that or wrote that." This is where accountability for your work begins.

In the case of Pat, perhaps Pat had no prior knowledge of Cuba, its culture, language, and location. In this situation, Pat can improve comprehension by increasing extralinguistic knowledge or world knowledge. By carefully using the follow-up process, Pat can see that it is important to have a broader range of information and also a larger vocabulary. The word belie is a new vocabulary word for Pat.

Step 5 **Action**

Develop a plan for action based on analysis and assessment.

In the fifth step you review what you have discovered about your work in steps 1 through 4 and make decisions about what steps you would like to take next to improve your performance. Throughout the workbook, action plans are suggested, and you may think of other action plans on your own or with your teacher

The five-step follow-up of self-assessment is unprecedented in interpreter education, so don't worry if you find it unfamiliar. By developing accurate self-assessment skills, you also develop control over the parts of the interpretation process that should be under the interpreter's control.

As a result of the follow-up process, Pat realizes that understanding words is not enough to ensure comprehension and that to increase the number of words Pat can rely on, it is important to get a thesaurus. Pat knows now that it is important to be aware of various cultures and of how cultural information can influence a person. Pat has also gained information regarding the location of Cuba and the University of Florida that will increase his extralinguistic knowledge. Even though this is a short speech, Pat has gained a deeper insight into the process of comprehension and realizes that by putting extra effort into tracking down information, the process of comprehension can be improved. By using the follow-up for all of the exercises, Pat can more than double the effectiveness of current cognitive processing skill levels.

Five-Step Follow-up

The purpose of the follow-up is to give you the opportunity to examine your own work, analyze its strong and weak points and make decisions about specific next steps in your study and practice efforts.

Step 1 **Observation**

This step allows you to observe your work objectively. Review your answers to the study questions.

Step 2 **Selection**

Mark the lines on the transcript that contain information that you did not fully understand when you first heard it.

Step 3 **Analysis**

Compare your work with the printed transcript, and the DVD. After you have read the transcript, see if you gained additional information by reading what you missed while listening. Write down any instances of this. Compare your comprehension based on listening only with your comprehension based on reading while listening.

Step 4 **Assessment**

Look for underlying reasons for successes or errors. For example, were there any noises or movements in the room that may have distracted you while you were listening?

____

____

____

Step 5 **Action**

Develop a plan for action based on your analysis and assessment.

____

____

____

EXERCISE 1.2

Growing Up in New York City

EUGENE CORBETT

Directions

In this exercise, it will take approximately four minutes to listen to the selection. After you have listened to the selection, answer the study questions, then do the follow-up. Find a quiet place to work where you will not be interrupted. Find this selection on your DVD. Adjust the volume as necessary. Be sure you can see the screen clearly. Begin by allowing yourself time to focus on the speaker's face. Listen to Eugene Corbett's description of growing up in New York City. Do not write while listening. You do not need to record your answers on video or audiotape. After watching this selection, answer the study questions below in the space provided.

Study Questions

1. Use a dictionary to look up any new words. Find synonyms for as many words as you can. What is a borough? Did you notice that Eugene Corbett said there were five and mentioned only four? What is the fifth one?

2. Is Eugene Corbett an identical twin or a fraternal twin? How do you know which he is? When did his parents pass away?

3. Eugene Corbett says that his family moved to "the projects." What does that mean?

4. What is pfiesteria and how does it affect fish?

5. List other features of the description that you would like to look up. For example, where are the NYC boroughs located in relation to each other? What are the names of the five boroughs?

6. What does the speaker mean when he says his son Eugene is 14 and thinks he is 43?

Transcript for *Growing Up in New York City*, Eugene Corbett

Hello. My name is Eugene Corbett. I'd like to give you a little history about my experie—experiences growing up in New York City as young adult and juvenile. I was born in the Bronx, New York, and as you know, New York City has five boroughs: Manhattan, Queens, Brooklyn and Manhattan. I grew up in Bronx. My mother's name was Vivian Corbett and my father's name was Eugene Corbett. I attended the elementary school in the Bronx, which was PS 18. I enjoyed going to school there. Having been an only child I didn't have anyone to play with. I am a twin; my sister passed away when she was approximately nine months of age. They told me that she had pneumonia. Of course, playing by yourself as a child was not that fun, but I couldn't get anyone to take my blame for the mistakes I made. So I had to make my own mistakes and get blamed for them. But it was fun anyway.

My parents moved to the projects after I finished elementary school. And there we moved and I had my own room for the first time. I enjoyed putting things on the wall and placing toys all over the place. It was a lot of fun. I attended junior high school also in the Bronx, and there I enjoyed different sports activities. I also went to school in the Bronx high school, which is Evander Childs High School. As a student there I attended various types of activities, such as swimming, track and tennis. I enjoyed tennis the most. I never was famous but I enjoyed it anyway.

Several years later I was married to a young lady named Constance Knight in 1972. The marriage didn't last very long; I was very young.

Soon after my divorce I moved to Washington, DC, to become a federal law enforcement officer. I attended Howard University School of Social Work, where I obtained my Master's degree in Social Work.

It's a very rewarding career. In 1984 I was appointed as a United States probation officer for the District of Columbia. I am now serving in that capacity. It has been a very rewarding and a very enjoyable experience. I wish my parents was alive today just to see the success that I have achieved over the years.

I'm currently married to Suzanne Blackman Corbett. I have two wonderful children: Vivian, age 9, and Eugene, age 14, who thinks he's 43. However, I have a full hand on him. I enjoy my family. We do a lot of camping during the summer. I enjoy going fishing, even though fishing hasn't been great recently, due to a disease called pfiesteria. But hopefully next year things will be better. I enjoy family outings and activities. I'm a member of the Boy Scouts, Troop 1669 as well as my son. Recently last week we went camping in the rain for three days. Of course I caught a cold but I'm fine now. Scouting is a very enjoyable organization activity, and I certainly encourage everyone to join. I'm also a member of Ebeneezer Church in this area, and I try—I find that church is a very rewarding and spiritual uplift to help me in the community.

Five-Step Follow-up

Step 1 Observation

Review your answers to the study questions. Listen to the selection again and read the transcript.

Step 2 Selection

Listen to the selection again while reading the transcript. Circle any portions of the transcript where you did not fully understand the message the first time you heard it.

Step 3 Analysis

Refer to your answer to step 2. Review your work and determine the reasons that you did or did not understand the message the first time you heard it.

Step 4 **Assessment**

Refer to your answer to step 3. Did your background knowledge help you to understand? Why or why not? Did errors in comprehension occur when your attention shifted away from the speaker? How can you improve your concentration while listening?

Step 5 **Action**

Develop a plan for action based on your analysis and assessment. For example, if you noticed that you gained more information by reading than by listening, you may want to devote additional time to practicing with prerecorded spoken texts. Then you can listen to them a second or third time to be sure that you are listening carefully enough to enhance your comprehension skills.

EXERCISE 1.3

The Gift

BOBBI JORDAN

Directions

It will take approximately five minutes to listen to the selection. Then answer the study questions and do the follow-up. Find a quiet place to work where you will not be interrupted. Find this selection on your DVD. Adjust the volume as necessary. Be sure you can see the screen clearly. Begin by allowing yourself time to focus on the speaker's face. Listen to Bobbi Jordan talk about the gift. Do not write while listening. You do not need to record your answers on video or audiotape. After watching this selection, answer the study questions below in the space provided.

Study Questions

1. Use a dictionary to look up any new words. Find synonyms for as many words as you can.

   ____

   ____

   ____

   ____

2. What is the speaker's intent in giving this talk?

   ____

   ____

3. What does the phrase "tile person" mean?

   ____

What does "brought that church to life" mean?

What is sage green?

What does "scrimp and save" mean?

What is a rectory?

4. What does "lost her son" mean?

How old was Annie's son?

Who is Aunt Tillie?

5. Bobbi Jordan says this story changed her life. How did it change her life?

Transcript for *The Gift*, Bobbi Jordan

Hi. My name is Bobbi Jordan, and I'd like to tell you a story that changed my life. When I first came to California I had a very good friend who lived in a tiny community and she's the person who told me this story, so I have it second-hand. At that time, a young priest came to that community; and we're going to call him by the name of John. It was a small community and they were thrilled to have a young priest with new ideas who was an exciting person and brought that Catholic church to life. The community was so happy about this that they got together and they redid the parish hall. The men who were carpenters put new wood into the house, and the plumbers redid the plumbing, and one man was a tile person so the bathroom was tiled in a beautiful sage green tile, and the community went out of its way to make this a wonderful living place for this young priest.

Well, my friend, who was married with three young children and had a husband who had a small business, didn't have a lot of money. She didn't work. And so she had to scrimp and to save from her grocery money and from other money coming in to give her present to the priest for the rectory. She bought towels for the bathroom. She went shopping until she found *exactly* the right shade of green, and they were *very* expensive towels and she was so proud of her gift; and wrapped it carefully and took it to him. And said, "Here, Father, this is my gift for the rectory." He smiled, he was very pleased, and he knew that she was giving him the gift out of love.

About a year later, my friend went to Annie's house. Annie was a woman who had just lost her son, and so all the women in the community were taking casseroles and giving comfort because the son was a young boy and Annie was quite depressed. While my friend was there she went into Annie's bathroom; and hanging in the bathroom were the very towels that she had bought for the priest! She looked at them and couldn't believe her eyes—she knew they weren't Annie's. Annie didn't have any money, and besides, Annie's bathroom was salmon—who would have picked green towels? She went back out and she didn't say a word to Annie. Instead, the next day she went to the rectory, knocked on the door, had a small conversation with Father, and then said, "I don't understand. I was over at Annie's yesterday, and I saw the towels that I gave you hanging in her bathroom." Father said, "Yes, that's right." My friend said, "But I worked hard for those—and I saved my money and I scrimped and I saved so I could give you this gift!" Father looked her in the eye and said, "But, my dear, Annie *needed* them."

And that's when I had that wonderful recognition that only comes once in a lifetime. That there was a great lesson to be learned here; and the lesson is this: When you give a gift, it is gone. You give it, you give it to the person that you love, and then you let go of it. You let it be. If that person, be it your Aunt Tillie, your best friend, wants to take that gift and give it away the *very next day,* that's just fine—because you have given, not the object, but your love. That was an important lesson for me to learn that day, and that's my story.

Five-Step Follow-up

Step 1 Observation

Review your answers to the study questions. Listen to the selection again and read the transcript.

Step 2 **Selection**

Circle any parts of the transcript that contain information that you did not fully understand when you heard it.

Step 3 **Analysis**

Refer to your answer to step 2. Review your work and determine the reasons that you did or did not understand the message when you heard it.

____

____

____

____

Step 4 **Assessment**

Refer to your answer to step 3. Did your background knowledge help you to understand? Why or why not? Did errors in comprehension occur when your attention shifted away from the speaker? How can you improve your concentration while listening?

____

____

____

____

Step 5 **Action**

Develop a plan for action based on your analysis and assessment.

For example, if you noticed that you gained more information by reading than by listening, you may want to devote additional time to practicing with prerecorded, spoken texts. Listen to them a second or third time to be sure that you are listening carefully enough to enhance your comprehension skills. For an action plan you might listen carefully to how people tell stories that have a moral. Where does the moral of the story usually occur?

____

____

Progress Tracking Sheet

This sheet is designed to help you keep track of which exercises you have completed and how well you have done on these exercises. See page 12 for a full description of how to use the Progress Tracking Sheet.

Exercise Number	Date	First Performance	Study Questions	Follow-up Activity	Questions and Reminders	Date	Second Performance
Exercise 1.1 Quantitative							
Qualitative							
Exercise 1.2 Quantitative							
Qualitative							
Exercise 1.3 Quantitative							
Qualitative							
Quantitative Totals							

UNIT 2

Memory

Introduction

Interpreters must be able to accurately remember the content of the source message long enough to process it into the TL. Schweda-Nicholson (1996) has written a critical review of the recent literature dealing with the role of memory in interpretation. She reviews a number of theories including those of Atkinson and Shiffrin (1968). They proposed a model of human memory that indicates sensory information, once perceived, is held in short-term memory for recall. Their hypothesis suggests that this kind of information is held phonemically and is lost if not rehearsed soon after it arrives.

Schweda-Nicholson goes on to provide a summary of short-term memory, which is also known as working memory. The duration of working memory is thought to be only 250 milliseconds, which is a very short amount of time. According to Baddeley (1990) there are three parts to working memory. The first is the central executive, which controls working memory. The second is the visuo–spatial sketchpad, which is the place where mental images are probably created and stored. The third part is the articulatory loop, which can retain limited amounts of information. The combination of these three aspects of working memory combine to allow interpreters to use visualization and other strategies to assist the working memory aspects of the interpretation process.

In addition to working or short-term memory there is long-term memory. Schweda-Nicholson points out that long-term memory has two broad categories, procedural memory and propositional memory. Procedural memory is used to perform actions such as typing or rollerblading after they have been learned. It is no longer necessary to think of each step in the process. Propositional memory is the memory that allows a person to remember concepts. Propositional memory can be further subdivided. Propositional memory has two main components according to Tulvig (1983). The first is episodic memory, which allows people to remember events from their own lifetimes. The second is semantic memory, which is general knowledge that is retained, regardless of how it was learned.

Schweda-Nicholson (1996) points out the relevance of procedural memory to interpretation. This is the kind of memory that is evoked without conscious awareness. "It has been suggested that much of the process of interpretation (especially simultaneous) becomes almost automatic with practice. In other words, the procedural knowledge necessary for accomplishing the task of SI is activated independently and unconsciously, thereby leaving the bulk of attentional resources available for semantic analysis of incoming source language material as well as formulation output and monitoring of the target language rendition" (p. 102). This means that even though the process of simultaneous interpretation (SI) is very complex and demanding, some aspects of it can become less effortful. However, the two aspects that will almost always require high levels of effort are determining what is meant by the incoming message and formulating the outgoing message. One of the key factors in being able to analyze the incoming message is memory. It is vital that the incoming message be remembered long enough to be analyzed.

The Role of Memory in the Interpretation Process

Interpreters are generally not responsible for remembering the content of messages that they have interpreted after they are finished interpreting. However, memory is an important part of the interpretation process. The various components of working memory and long term-memory are important for interpreters. Experienced interpreters tend to shift quickly and efficiently between working memory and long-term memory stores without conscious realization. Schweda-Nicholson emphasizes that there is a constant interplay between working and long-term memory during the interpretation process. It is as if interpreters can quickly access what they know about a topic and tap into that knowledge to help them process the incoming message.

General world knowledge falls into the category of long-term memory. Gile (1995) refers to this kind of knowledge as extralinguistic knowledge (ELK). The more you know, or remember about a topic, the better when it comes to interpretation. This is part of why it is easier to interpret a speech when the topic is familiar. Because ELK is so valuable for interpreters, they often feel it is very important to read daily newspapers and be as well educated as possible.

If memory skills are well developed, there is a much higher chance that the resulting interpretation will be accurate. It may be that developing and practicing a specific processing skill such as auditory memory, leads to increased effectiveness in the interpretation process. Certainly, practice in specific skills can cause those skills to become more automatic. While the type of working-memory processes required for interpretation could never be fully automatic, it is worthwhile to at least reduce the amount of effort required.

Gile (1995) suggests that interpretation requires a certain amount of "mental energy" and that the requirements of the interpretation task must not exceed the interpreter's available supply of mental energy. When the demands of the job exceed the interpreter's mental energy, the interpretation performance will suffer. This idea of limited supplies of mental energy adds support to the notion that it is worthwhile to reduce the amount of effort associated with specific parts of the interpretation process. Often this effort can be reduced by practice on the component parts of the interpretation process so that the components become more nearly automatic.

Memory Exercises

EXERCISE 2.1

Introduction

MAUREEN LEWNES

Directions

It will take approximately one minute to listen to the selection. Then answer the study questions and do the follow-up. Find a quiet place to work where you will not be interrupted. Find this selection on your DVD. Adjust the volume as necessary. Be sure you can see the screen clearly. Begin by allowing yourself time to focus on the speaker's face. Listen to Maureen Lewnes's introduction. Do not write while listening. You do not need to record your answers on video or audiotape. After watching this selection, answer the study questions in the space provided.

Study Questions

1. Write down all the details you can remember about Maureen Lewnes.

2. Listen to the DVD again while reading the transcript and put circles around any details that you may have missed.

3. Were any of the vocabulary items unfamiliar? Write them down and consult a dictionary to look up the meanings.

4. To increase your ELK, look on a map to locate San Diego. Poway is a suburb of San Diego. Does it appear on your map?

5. What strategies did you use to focus your listening on the speaker's message? What strategies did you use to remember what you heard?

Transcript for *Introduction,* Maureen Lewnes

Hello. My name is Maureen Lewnes. I'm from San Diego, California. I'm a wife, a mother, and a schoolteacher. I teach elementary school in Poway, California, and I teach upper elementary, uh, grade children in grades four and five.

Five-Step Follow-up

Step 1 Observation

Review your answers to the study questions.

Step 2 Selection

Refer to your answer to Study Question 2. The brackets indicate the portions of the selection that you did not remember accurately.

Step 3 Analysis

Analyze for accuracy.

After you have read the transcript, see if you gained additional information by reading what you missed while listening. Underline any information that you missed while listening.

Step 4 **Assessment**

Look for underlying reasons for successes or errors.

Did your background knowledge help you to understand? Why or why not? What happened if your attention was not focused on the speaker's message?

____

____

____

____

Step 5 **Action**

Develop a plan for action based on your analysis and assessment.

For example, when you hear a city or place name that you do not know, such as Poway, what strategies do you use to remember that new word? If you do not have a strategy to deal with words that are new to you, develop a strategy for your action plan.

____

____

____

____

EXERCISE 2.2

Introduction

PETER LEARY

Directions

It will take approximately one minute to listen to the selection. Then answer the study questions and do the follow-up. Find a quiet place to work where you will not be interrupted. Find this selection on your DVD. Adjust the volume as necessary. Be sure you can see the screen clearly. Begin by allowing yourself time to focus on the speaker's face. Listen to Peter Leary's introduction. Do not write while listening. You do not need to record your answers on video or audiotape. After watching this selection, answer the study questions in the space provided.

Study Questions

1. Write down all the details you can remember about Peter Leary.

____

____

____

____

____

____

2. Listen to the DVD again while reading the transcript and put circles around any details that you may have missed.

3. Were any of the vocabulary words unfamiliar? Write them down and consult a dictionary. Check a thesaurus for other words that could be used.

4. To increase your ELK, look on a map or the World Wide Web to locate the University of California at Davis.

Why would San Diego be a great place to live?

5. What strategies did you use to focus your listening on the speaker's message? What strategies did you use to remember what you heard?

Transcript for *Introduction* Peter Leary

Hello. I'm Peter Leary, but my grandpa calls me Peter Joseph. I've lived in San Diego with my two brothers, my two sisters, and my two parents for my whole life, and San Diego's—you know, it's a great place to live and I've had a good time—had a good life. Aah, right now I'm a student and next year I'm going to be a freshman at UC—University of California at Davis, and I'm really looking forward to it: there's a lot of people up there, a lot of good chances to make friends, learn new things. It should be a good experience. Planning on double majoring in biology and history, eventually becoming a doctor. Probably an oncologist—someone dealing with cancer and cancer patients. Other than that, I like to swim, I like to play water polo, I like to kayak, I like to do things outdoors. And that pretty much is me.

Five-Step Follow-up

Step 1 Observation

Review your answers to the study questions.

Step 2 Selection

Refer to your answer to Study Question 2. The circles indicate sections you did not remember accurately.

Step 3 Analysis

After you have read the transcript, underline any additional information learned by reading that you missed while listening.

Step 4 Assessment

Look for underlying reasons for successes or errors.

Did your background knowledge help you to understand? Why or why not? What happened if your attention was not focused on the speaker's message?

____

____

____

____

Step 5 Action

Develop a plan for action based on your analysis and assessment.

For example, look up any words that you did not remember correctly such as the word *oncologist,* in your dictionary. This may help you remember its meaning more easily the next time you hear it. If you did not remember any parts of the autobiography, try to decide what you can do to improve your listening strategies to improve memory. Some examples might be to practice listening with your eyes closed. If that helps, then you must move quickly to listening more intently with your eyes open. You can also clear your mind of personal matters and focus closely on the speaker's face.

____

____

____

____

EXERCISE 2.3

Kidnapped

PETER LEARY

Directions

It will take approximately three minutes to listen to the selection. Then answer the study questions and do the follow-up. Find a quiet place to work where you will not be interrupted. Find this selection on your DVD. Adjust the volume as necessary. Be sure you can see the screen clearly. Begin by allowing yourself time to focus on the speaker's face. Listen to Peter Leary's story. Do not write while listening. You do not need to record your answers on video or audiotape. After watching this selection, answer the study questions in the space provided.

Study Questions

1. Write down all the details that you can remember in the order that they happened in *Kidnapped.*

   Friend knocks on window. He goes to door to say good morning. All the sudden bunch people in black masks jump out and blindfold him, tie him up and throw him back seat of car. Drive around town. Music comes on. Then car stops. People get out. He's about to fall back asleep. People come back open trunk, take him out, lead him into woods. Through blindfold he can see light looks like fire. When there, blindfold off, birthday cake, big group of friends and family party for his birthday.

2. Listen to the DVD again while reading the transcript and put circles around any details that you may not have remembered.

3. Refer to your answer to question 1. Compare your answer to question 1 with the transcript of *Kidnapped.* Check to see if you have maintained the order of events. If not, underline the parts of the transcript where you misremembered the order of events.

4. What strategies did you use to remember the speaker's message?

   Watching face as well as listening to what he was saying.

5. If you did not remember some parts of *Kidnapped,* determine if those parts were central to the message or if they were supporting details. List supporting details.

Transcript for *Kidnapped,* Peter Leary

Hello. I'm Peter Leary and this is my story. I want you to picture a group of your closest friends. Now picture yourself asleep in bed, 1:00 in the morning, on the morning of your eighteenth birthday. Got the picture? Good. Picture your best friend knockin' on the window, jerkin' you awake, and you blink your eyes a coupla times, clear the sleep, see 'em out there, walk to your front door and you step outside, about ready to say "top of the morning to you" to your good friend. And suddenly, out of the woodwork jump a whole bunch of people wearing black with masks on, tie your hands behind your back, and take you out to a car, throw you in the back seat. You picture? Good. Well, anyway, they're drivin' around takin' you over every speed bump, every sharp corner in the city and, basically just takin' you all over the place—you have a blindfold on, you can't see anything. You're wondering what's goin' on. The radio starts to play, head's right next to the speaker—all in all, it's not a bad time, but you've just been kidnapped by your friends. You picture? Good. Well, eventually they go, they park somewhere, pull over to the side of the road, and they all get out of the car. You're still in there, and right about when you think you're gonna slip off back to sleep, they come back, open up the door, pull you out and begin taking you into the woods. Through your blindfold you can see the light. It's kinda like a fire, it looks like, and they're takin' you over there, they take off the blindfold, and what do you know—it's a big birthday cake. Everyone's all around, singin' Happy Birthday, havin' a good time, and ah, you've been kidnapped on the morning of your birthday—thrown in a car, and taken into the forest for this birthday cake. That didn't happen to you. That happened to me.

Five-Step Follow-up

Step 1 Observation

Review your answers to the study questions.

Step 2 Selection

Refer to your answer to Study Question 2. The circles indicate sections you did not remember accurately. The underlined areas indicate areas where you misremembered the order of events.

Step 3 Analysis

After you have read the transcript; put parentheses around any additional information learned by reading that you missed while listening.

Step 4 Assessment

Look for underlying reasons for successes or errors.

Did your background knowledge help you to understand? Why or why not? What happened if your attention was not focused on the speaker's message?

____

____

____

____

Step 5 Action

Develop a plan for action based on your analysis and assessment.

For example, there were many scenes that could be visualized in *Kidnapped.* Did you try to remember the words in the story or did you rely on the visual images in your mind? In a story like this one, using your visuo–spatial sketchpad will help improve your memory for the main ideas and supporting ideas. Practice using a visuo–spatial sketchpad while you are listening to other selections.

____

____

____

____

Progress Tracking Sheet

This sheet is designed to help you keep track of which exercises you have completed and how well you have done on these exercises. See page 12 for a full description of how to use the Progress Tracking Sheet.

Exercise Number	Date	First Performance	Study Questions	Follow-up Activity	Questions and Reminders	Date	Second Performance
Exercise 2.1 Quantitative							
Qualitative							
Exercise 2.2 Quantitative							
Qualitative							
Exercise 2.3 Quantitative							
Qualitative							
Quantitative Totals							

UNIT 3 Acuity and Discrimination

Introduction

Acuity means acuteness of perception. If you can't clearly perceive the source message, you will not be able to process or remember it. Discrimination, in this context, means the ability to perceive distinguishing features in spoken English. It is important for interpreters to be able to remember differences in source texts that may be similar to each other, but not identical. A real life example of the need for acuity and discrimination would be when the interpreter interprets the same tour or type of meeting frequently. The topic and context may be similar, but there may be differences in the content.

Memory and comprehension together play an important role in acuity and discrimination because first the message must be remembered and understood, then the distinguishing features can be noticed. Important aspects of acuity and discrimination can be improved by practice in developing focused listening and analysis skills.

The Role of Acuity and Discrimination in the Interpretation Process

Acuity and discrimination skills are a crucial and often overlooked component of interpreter education. Interpreters must be able to hear differences in English words, especially in contexts that may be similar, such as a lecture given by the same speaker on two different occasions. This lecture may contain the same basic information but may have some important differences in content or order of information. Interpreters need to be able to distinguish homonyms, or words that sound the same, by listening carefully to the context in which the words occur. For example, acuity and discrimination skills will assist the interpreter in knowing which meaning is intended when hearing "Do you have a pair?" or "Do you have a pear?". For example, when people introduce themselves, they may say similar things about themselves each time, but there could be differences in word order.

Students of interpretation need to devote time and practice to the development of the skill of focused listening for differences in meaning, intonation, and order of information. Ordinary listening does not require the level of focused listening that is needed in the interpretation process. One way to improve focused listening for differences in spoken English is through practice in acuity and discrimination drills. This unit provides practice in this kind of discrimination. The exercises in this unit provide specific practice in focused listening with the goal of improving acuity and discrimination.

Acuity and Discrimination Exercises

EXERCISE 3.1

Two Introductions

AMY BOUCK

Directions

Find this selection on your DVD. Adjust the volume as necessary. Be sure you can see the screen clearly. Begin by allowing yourself time to focus on the speaker's face. Read the study questions before you listen to the selection. It will take approximately two minutes to listen to the selection. Then answer the study questions and do the follow-up. Find a quiet place to work where you will not be interrupted.

Listen to Amy Bouck's introductions, Versions A and B. Do not write while listening. You do not need to record your answers on video or audiotape. After watching this selection, answer the study questions in the space provided.

Study Questions

1. Make a list of any differences in content, vocabulary, or order of information between Version A and Version B.

___

___

___

___

2. Refer to the transcript and put parentheses around any differences that you heard in Version B that did not occur in Version A.

___

___

___

3. Are any details mentioned in only one introduction? What are those details and in which introduction do they appear?

___

___

4. Read the transcripts and look for examples where different words are used to express the same idea. Put brackets around any differences in vocabulary.

5. Read the transcripts and underline examples of differences in the order of information.

6. Do any of the differences that you have noted create a difference in mean-

ing? Write down examples that show how the meaning was changed by the differences that you noticed in word order or in order of information.

____

____

Transcript for *Introduction Version A,* Amy Bouck

Hi. My name is Amy Bouck. I'm 20 years old. I'm originally from San Diego, California. I now live in Davis, California, which is about 20 minutes outside Sacramento. I study up there at the University of California at Davis; I'm studying psychology... um, when I'm not studying, some of the things I like to do include camping, watching TV, shopping and reading books. Uh, and that's all about me.

Transcript for *Introduction Version B,* Amy Bouck

Hi. My name is Amy Bouck. I'm 20 years old. I'm originally from San Diego, California. I now live in northern California, in Davis, which is about 20 minutes outside Sacramento. I study at the University of California at Davis up there; I'm studying psychology. When I'm not studying I enjoy doing things like reading books, watching TV, going shopping and camping. And that's all about me.

Five-Step Follow-up

Step 1 Observation

Review your answers.

Step 2 Selection

Read the transcripts and compare your answer to question 1 with the transcripts. Circle the line numbers for the portions of the introductions where you notice differences between your answers to question 1 and the transcript.

Step 3 **Analysis**

Reread the transcripts to check for any other differences in content, vocabulary, and order of information that you notice between Introduction A and B. Note the line numbers of those differences in the transcripts. Your analysis should include the following categories: new information, different order of information, and different word choices. Did you notice these differences as you listened to the speeches?

Step 4 **Assessment**

Look for underlying reasons that allowed you to notice these small differences the first time you heard the selections. Did your background knowledge help you to understand? Why or why not? What happened if your attention was not focused on the speaker's message? Did what you heard in Introduction A interfere with your ability to accurately listen to Introduction B?

____

____

____

____

Step 5 **Action**

Develop a plan for action based on your analysis and assessment.

For example, do you need to focus your listening more intently when you hear the same person talk about the same topic more than once? An action plan could include practicing acuity and discrimination skills by listening to the same radio announcer or television newscaster introduce himself for several days in a row. Notice if the announcer says exactly the same thing in the same order each day. Find other examples of spoken information that is repeated often and see if you notice differences between repetitions.

____

____

____

____

____

EXERCISE 3.2

Trip to the Hospital

AMY BOUCK

Directions

Find this selection on your DVD. Adjust the volume as necessary. Be sure you can see the screen clearly. Begin by allowing yourself time to focus on the speaker's face. Read the study questions before you listen to the selection. It will take approximately three and a half minutes to listen to the selection. After listening, answer the study questions and do the follow-up. Find a quiet place to work where you will not be interrupted.

Listen to Amy Bouck describe both versions of her trip to the hospital. Do not write while listening. You do not need to record your answers on video or audiotape. After watching this selection, answer the study questions.

Study Questions

1. Based solely on what you heard, make a list of any differences in content, vocabulary, or order of information between Version A and Version B.

   ____

   ____

   ____

2. Refer to the transcript and put parentheses around any differences that you heard between Versions A and B in content.

3. Read the transcript and put brackets around differences in vocabulary between Versions A and B.

4. Read the transcript and underline any differences in order of information. Are any details mentioned in only one of the versions? What are those details and in which version do they appear? Did you assume that both

versions would have the same details?

5. Do any of the differences that you have noted create a difference in meaning? Write down instances of where the meaning was changed by the differences that you noticed in word order or order of information.

Transcript for *Trip to the Hospital Version A*, Amy Bouck

Hi. My name is Amy Bouck, and I'm gonna tell you about when I was five years old and had to go to the hospital. I'd come down with a stomach flu, so my mom took me to the doctor and he said that I just had to stick it out and wait to get better. Uh, but I continued to get worse so my mom took me to another doctor and that doctor agreed with the first that I just had to stick it out and get better. A week had passed, and I continued to get worse so my mom took me to the emergency room. I was examined by a doctor, and he said that I had to have my appendix out. So he called an ambulance and I was rushed down to the, uh, emergency room at the naval hospital and—where I was examined, and they agreed with the previous doctor that I had to get my appendix out. So I was admitted to the children's ward of the hospital, where, uh, I had to change into a full gown and I had a bed, and then I was operated on at 1:00 that morning. Uh, the worst part was I had to spend my birthday in the hospital.

Transcript for *Trip to the Hospital Version B*, Amy Bouck

Hi. My name is Amy Bouck, and I'm gonna tell you about when I was five years old and had to go to the hospital. I'd come down with the stomach flu and my mom was worried about me, so she took me to the doctor. He said that I just had to wait to get better and stick it out. I continued to get worse and so my mom took me to another doctor, who said the same thing—that I had to just wait to get better. But I continued to get worse, so my mom brought me to the emergency room.

The doctor examined me and he said that I had to have my appendix taken out. He called an ambulance for me, which took me to the hospital, where I was examined again. That doctor also said I had to have my appendix out. So I was admitted to the children's ward of the hospital, where they suited me up in a gown and gave me a bed. I was operated at 1:00 that morning. I had to stay in the hospital for six days to recover, where I had to do exercises like walk around the hospital or uh, be hooked up to something to test how deep I could breathe—all helping me to get better. Uh, one of the worst parts about being in the hospital was I had to celebrate my birthday there. But all my family came to visit me, and gave me things like candy and posters. But all the doctors took my candy. And, uh, that's my trip to the hospital.

Five-Step Follow-up

Step 1 Observation

Review your answers to the study questions.

Step 2 Selection

Refer to your answer to Study Question 1, which was based on what you could remember after listening and compare it to your answers to questions 3 and 4. Circle the line numbers for the portions of the introductions where you notice differences between your answers to Study Question 1 and the transcript.

Step 3 Analysis

Reread the transcripts to check for any other differences in content, vocabulary, and order of information that you notice between Versions A and B. Note the line numbers of those differences in the transcripts. Your analysis should include the following categories, new information, different order of information, and different word choices. Did you notice these differences as you listened to the speeches or did you notice them only after you read the transcript?

____

____

____

____

Step 4 Assessment

Look for underlying reasons that allowed you to notice these differences the first time you heard the selections. Did the speaker's rate of speech affect your acuity and discrimination? Did what you heard in Version A interfere with what you heard in Version B?

____

____

____

Step 5 Action

Develop a plan for action based on your analysis and assessment.

For example, plan to focus your listening more intently when you hear the same person talk about the same topic more than once. An action plan could include asking a friend to tell a short story (three minutes) from childhood and to repeat it twice. Record all three versions of the short story. Then use the study questions to help you analyze your work.

EXERCISE 3.3

Three Introductions

LORRAINE OLDHAM

Directions

Find this selection on your DVD. Adjust the volume as necessary. Be sure you can see the screen clearly. Begin by allowing yourself time to focus on the speaker's face. Read the study questions before you listen to the selection. It will take approximately three minutes to listen to the selection. After listening to the selection, answer the study questions and do the follow-up. Find a quiet place to work where you will not be interrupted.

Listen to Lorraine Oldham's introductions, Versions A, B, and C. Do not write while listening. You do not need to record your answers on video or audiotape. After watching this selection, answer the study questions in the space provided.

Study Questions

1. Based solely on what you heard, make a list of any differences in content, vocabulary, or order of information between Versions A and B.

____

2. Refer to the transcript and put parentheses around any differences in content that you heard between Versions A and B.

3. Are any details mentioned in only one version? What are those details and in which version do they appear?

____

____

4. Read the transcripts and look for examples where different words are used to express the same idea. Put brackets around any differences in vocabulary.

5. Read the transcripts and underline any differences in the order of information.

6. Do any of the differences that you have noted create a difference in meaning? Write down instances of where the meaning was changed by the differences that you noticed in word order or order of information.

____

____

____

7. Put parentheses around any differences in content that appear only in C. Put brackets around any vocabulary that appears in C but not in A or B.Underline any differences in order of information that appear only in C.

Transcript for *Introduction, Version A,* Lorraine Oldham

Hi. I'm Lorraine Oldham. I was born and raised in Long Island, New York. I came to San Diego in 1970 with my husband and young son and had three additional children after that and raised them here in San Diego up until '91 when we moved back to Boston, Massachusetts. And we lived there for just about five years and really had a hard time adjusting to the cold weather, so we returned here to San Diego just about a year ago. And we're glad to be back with long-time friends and neighbors and also our family. Our children are grown now and I have two small grandchildren that I'm really proud of. And I'm really glad to be here in San Diego again.

Transcript for *Introduction, Version B,* Lorraine Oldham

Hello. I'm Lorraine Oldham. I was born and raised in Long Island, New York and have come a long way to San Diego, California. We moved here in 1970 with one small child and my husband and our pet, Laddie. We raised three additional children here in San Diego up until 1991 when we moved back to Boston, Massachusetts. We had a hard time adjusting to the cold winters back there and were very anxious to get back here, and returned just about last year and are very happy to be back with long-time friends and neighbors and our family once again. It's great to be back in San Diego.

Transcript for *Introduction, Version C,* Lorraine Oldham

I'm Lorraine Oldham and I was born and raised in Long Island, New York. We came here to San Diego in 1970 with my husband, son, and our pet Laddie and we had three additional children while we lived here in San Diego up until 1991 and had to return to Boston,

Massachusetts. And we had a hard time adjusting to the cold weather there, and were very glad to return here to San Diego just about a year ago. And we're very glad to be here because we have our long-time friends once again with us, and our family, and it's really great to be back in San Diego.

Five-Step Follow-up

Step 1 Observation

Review your answers.

Step 2 Selection

Refer to your answer to Study Questions 1 and 2 and compare them to your answers to questions 3 and 4. Read the transcripts and compare your answers with the transcripts and circle the line numbers for the portions of the introductions where you notice differences between your answers and the transcript.

Step 3 Analysis

Analyze for accuracy.

Reread the transcripts to check for any other differences in content, vocabulary, and order of information that you notice between Introduction A and Introduction B. Note the line numbers of those differences in the transcripts. Your analysis should include the following categories: new information, different order of information, and different word choices. Did you notice these differences as you listened to the speeches?

Step 4 Assessment

Look for underlying reasons that allowed you to notice these differences the first time you heard the selections. Did the speaker's rate of speech affect your acuity and discrimination? Did what you heard in Version A interfere with what you heard in Versions B and C?

____

____

____

____

Step 5 **Action**

Develop a plan for action based on your analysis and assessment.

For example, plan to focus your listening more intently when you hear the same person talk about the same topic more than once. An action plan could include asking a friend to provide a one-minute introduction of himself and to repeat it twice. Record all three versions of the introduction and then use the study questions to guide your analysis of your acuity and discrimination practice on these three introductions.

____

____

____

____

Additional Exercises to Strengthen Skills Developed in Units 1, 2, and 3

Here are some additional exercises that can be used to strengthen comprehension, auditory memory, and acuity and discrimination skills in a group setting, such as an interpreter training class or study group.

Group Activity 1. Autobiography

Members of the group will take turns delivering a short autobiography of two minutes or less. These short speeches should be planned, but not rehearsed or written out in advance. Ideally, the speeches will also be videotaped. The first benefit of this exercise is that these short autobiographies provide more samples of spontaneous spoken English in a live rather than videotaped format. While one member of the group is the speaker, the other members of the group will be listeners. Listeners will use focused listening to enhance acuity and discrimination skills. Each listener will need his or her own audiotape recorder and blank tape to record the short speeches given by group members.

This activity has a second benefit. The group member who is giving the speech can also be provided with feedback on their spoken English skills. Specific areas to note include: ability to speak in complete sentences, ability to organize information verbally, ability to pronounce English words clearly enough to be understood by members of the group, ability to maintain eye contact, and ability to use appropriate vocal intonation while avoiding unnecessary body shifting or movement.

A discussion can be held after group members have had an opportunity to answer the study questions and do the five-step follow-up. Group discussions can be helpful in gaining precision in listening and remembering details. Then this exercise is repeated with other group members acting as speakers. The responsibility of speaking may rotate throughout the group as time permits.

Directions

Each group member will list between eight and ten autobiographical facts on a sheet of paper. Group members who are listeners will turn on their tape recorders and listen to the speaker. The listeners will not write while listening. The person selected as the speaker will not read from the list, but will try to include the facts listed. After the first version of the speaker's autobiography, the listeners will turn off their tape recorders and can write down on their own paper a list of salient points from the speaker's presentation. Then, the listeners will turn on their tape recorders and the same speaker will retell the autobiography. When the speaker is finished, the listeners will turn off their tape recorders and refer to the study questions.

Study Questions

1. Write down any differences in content, vocabulary and order of information that you notice between the telling and retelling of the autobiography.

____

____

____

____

2. Note any comprehension difficulties. Write down any vocabulary words you want to look up.

3. Note any auditory memory difficulties you experienced. Were there any numbers or names in the text? Did names or numbers, such as birth dates or addresses make it more difficult to remember the information that came after the numbers?

4. Write down any questions you have for the speaker regarding the presentation.

5. Make a list of your strong points in comprehension, memory, and acuity and discrimination. List one thing that you noticed as a result of this exercise that you would like to improve.

____

____

____

Checklist for Speaker Performance

- Speak in complete sentences.
- Organize information coherently. (Speech has a beginning, middle, and ending)
- Pronounce English words clearly enough to be understood by members of the group.
- Maintain eye contact with audience.
- Use appropriate vocal intonation.
- Avoid unnecessary body shifting or movement.

Five-Step Follow-up

Step 1 **Observation**

Review what you wrote immediately after listening to the speaker for the first and second time.

Step 2 **Selection**

Select from this list one aspect of your work that you would most like to improve.

Noticed major differences in content.
Noticed minor differences in content.
Can remember what the differences were.

Step 3 **Analysis**

Analyze for accuracy.

Listen to the audiotape or videotape of the speech. Pay particular attention to the aspect of your work that you selected in step 2. See if you gained additional information by hearing it again. If you find additional information, write it down.

____

____

____

____

Step 4 **Assessment**

Look for underlying reasons for successes or errors. Did your background knowledge help you to understand the presentation? Are you familiar with the usual kinds of information that people tend to include in their autobiographies? Does that expectation help you with comprehension, memory, or acuity and discrimination? Why or why not? What happened if your attention was not focused on the speaker's message?

____

____

____

____

Step 5 **Action**

Develop a plan for action based on your analysis and assessment.

For example, note the differences between information that is presented live and that which is presented on video. Interpreters will have to deal with both kinds of spoken English and will need equally good skills in listening to both kinds of presentations. Practice listening to both live and videotaped material for comprehension, memory, and acuity and discrimination.

____

____

____

____

Group Activity 2. Eyewitness Account

This activity follows the same format as Group Activity 1. Group members will take turns as speakers and listeners. The speaker will provide a detailed account of an actual event that he or she witnessed, such as a car crash, a chance meeting with an old friend, the description of an event where a famous person was present, arrival at a surprise party, or some other event.

Then, the speaker will retell the same account. These eyewitness accounts should be prepared in advance, but not written down, even in list form. These talks should be three to four minutes long. In order to get the length within this range, speakers will need to practice once in advance of the class presentation and time their remarks. The other members of the group will listen and watch the speaker. When the speaker is finished, the group members will answer the study questions.

A discussion can be held after group members have had an opportunity to answer the study questions. Group discussions can be helpful in gaining precision in listening and remembering details because one person may have heard information that another person missed. By discussing these differences, group members can assist each other in noticing important details. Then this exercise is repeated with other group members acting as speakers. The responsibility of speaking may rotate throughout the group as time permits.

This exercise can be used for providing commentary on the oral presentation skills of the speakers. To do this, follow the guidelines for speakers as listed in Group Activity 1.

Directions

The speaker will describe an eyewitness account. The other group members will listen and watch the speaker without writing. The speaker will retell the same account. Group members will listen and watch and then write down *only* the details or events that appeared in the retelling but not in the original telling of the account. At first, students can write the differences as soon as they hear them. After obtaining some experience with this exercise, listeners can write the differences after the speaker has finished the retelling. Group members will rely on comprehension, auditory memory, and auditory discrimination to find the differences between the telling and retelling of the eyewitness account. After listening to the retelling, answer the study questions.

Study Questions

1. Write down the differences you heard between Version A and Version B.

____

____

____

____

2. Are there differences in vocabulary, order of information, or content in the two versions of the speaker's presentation?

   ____

   ____

   ____

   ____

3. Are there any features that are heard in only one version? What were they, and in which version do they appear? Do any of the differences you noticed create a difference in meaning?

   ____

   ____

   ____

   ____

4. Write down any questions you have for the speaker regarding the presentation.

   ____

   ____

   ____

   ____

5. Make a list of your strong points in comprehension, memory, and acuity and discrimination. List one thing that you noticed as a result of this exercise that you would like to improve.

   ____

   ____

Five-Step Follow-up

Step 1 Observation

Review your work.

Step 2 Selection

Select from this list one aspect of your work that you would most like to improve.

Noticed major differences in content.
Noticed minor differences in content.
Can remember what the differences were.

Step 3 Analysis

Analyze for accuracy.

Listen to the audiotape or videotape of the speech. Pay particular attention to the aspect of your work that you selected in step 2. See if you gained additional information by hearing it again. If you find additional information, write it down.

Step 4 Assessment

Look for underlying reasons for successes or errors. Did your background knowledge help you to understand the presentation? Are you familiar with the speaker? Does your acquaintance with the speaker help you with comprehension, memory, or acuity and discrimination? Why or why not? What happened if your attention was not focused on the speaker's message?

Step 5 Action

Develop a plan for action based on your analysis and assessment.

For example, note the differences between information that is presented live and that which is presented on video. Interpreters will have to deal with both kinds of spoken English and will need equally good skills in listening to both kinds of presentations. Practice listening to both live and videotaped material for comprehension, memory, and acuity and discrimination.

Group Activity 3. Numbers

This activity follows the same format as Group Activity 1. Group members will take turns as speakers and listeners. The talks should emphasize and contain numbers. These talks should be three minutes. In order to get the length within this range, speakers will need to practice once in advance of the class presentation and time their remarks. The other members of the group will listen and watch the speaker. When the speaker is finished, the group members will answer the study questions. A discussion can be held after group members have had an opportunity to fill in the study guide and do the five-step follow-up. Group discussions can be helpful in gaining precision in listening and remembering details. Then this exercise is repeated with other group members acting as speakers. The responsibility of speaking may rotate throughout the group as time permits.

This exercise can be used for providing commentary on the oral presentation skills of the speakers. To do this, follow the guidelines for speakers as listed in Group Activity 1.

Videotaping both versions of each speaker will allow for easy comparison of the two versions.

Directions

Speakers will prepare short speeches of three minutes, which will include numbers such as dates, phone numbers, and addresses. The speaker should not write out the speech in advance, but should have the numbers used in the speech listed on paper to be referred to during the speech. In this case, other group members will write down the numbers as they hear them, rather than wait for the entire speech to be finished before writing. The speaker will retell the same short speech. Listeners will listen to the retelling and check to see if the numbers they wrote down the first time they heard the speech are correct. Group members will rely on comprehension, auditory memory, and auditory discrimination. After listening to the retelling, answer the study questions.

Study Questions

1. Verbally describe the differences you heard between Version A and Version B. Use a tape recorder to record your answers. Speak in complete sentences.
2. Are there differences in vocabulary, order of information, or content? Describe verbally and record your answers. Remember to speak in complete sentences.
3. Are there any features that are heard in only one version? What are they, and in which version do they appear? Taperecord your answers, being mindful of your own speech.
4. Did you find it more difficult to remember the numbers than to remember the facts? If so, why? Explain your answer.

   ____

   ____

   ____

   ____

5. Can you restate, from memory, any of the numbers? For example, if the speaker gave a phone number or birth date, can you repeat it now? Record your answers on your audiotape. If you cannot recall the numbers exactly, see if you can formulate a reasonable approximation. For example, "The speaker was born in the fifties and has a birthday in the spring." This kind of response, while not exact, will allow you to recall the gist of the message.

Five-Step Follow-up

Step 1 Observation

Review your work.

Step 2 Selection

Select from this list one aspect of your work that you would most like to improve.

Noticed major differences in content.
Noticed minor differences in content.
Can remember what the differences were.

Step 3 Analysis

Analyze for accuracy.

Listen to the audiotape or videotape of the speech. Pay particular attention to the aspect of your work that you selected in step 2. See if you gained additional information by hearing it again. If you find additional information, write it down.

____

____

____

____

Step 4 Assessment

Look for underlying reasons for successes or errors. Did your background knowledge help you to understand the presentation? Are you familiar with the speaker? Does your acquaintance with the speaker help you with comprehension, memory, or acuity and discrimination? Why or why not?

____

____

____

____

Step 5 Action

Develop a plan for action based on your analysis and assessment.

For example, ask a friend to record some short speeches with numbers in them. Practice focused listening to grasp the numbers. Try recalling if the number was over ten or below ten. See if your memory for numbers improves by visualizing the number as you hear it.

____

____

____

____

Progress Tracking Sheet

This sheet is designed to help you keep track of which exercises you have completed and how well you have done on these exercises. See page 12 for a full description of how to use the Progress Tracking Sheet.

Exercise Number	Date	First Performance	Study Questions	Follow-up Activity	Questions and Reminders	Date	Second Performance
Exercise 3.1 Quantitative							
Qualitative							
Exercise 3.2 Quantitative							
Qualitative							
Exercise 3.3 Quantitative							
Qualitative							
Quantitative Totals							

UNIT 4

Immediate Repetition

Introduction

Repetition means to say or perform again. Immediate repetition means to say or perform again without delay. This type of repetition starts as soon as the listener has heard enough of the message to begin repeating it. The ability to listen and repeat is one aspect of simultaneity. Simultaneity means that several things are happening at the same time. This is what happens during simultaneous interpretation; many things happen all at the same time. The speaker is speaking while the interpreter is listening, comprehending, transferring the message to another language, expressing the message in that other language, and monitoring for accuracy. Although this is an oversimplified description of the interpretation process, it illustrates the point that the interpreter must be able to successfully manage a number of cognitive tasks all at the same time.

Immediate repetition uncovers the ability to find the minimal distance behind the speaker and maintain that distance. The distance, in time, that separates the speaker's utterance and the repetition of that utterance by the interpreter is a subject of much interest in interpretation. This distance is called lag time, processing time, decalage, or ear–voice span. All these terms refer to how much time has elapsed between when the speaker said something and when the interpreter renders the interpretation of that same utterance. By practicing the skill of immediate repetition and, later, delayed repetition, interpreters can get the feel for what it is like to maintain enough cognitive control over their repetitions to stay immediately behind the speaker or a phrase behind the speaker. Later, during actual simultaneous interpretation, the ability to control the amount of processing time becomes a valuable asset for the interpreter.

The ability to do immediate repetition includes self-monitoring. In this context, self-monitoring means that the interpreters listen to themselves while they are repeating to see if they are saying what the speaker said. Generally people can listen to themselves while repeating and know if they are repeating correctly or not. In this type of repetition, however, there is no real opportunity for corrections when an error is detected, due to time constraints.

Lambert (1989) calls immediate repetition *phonemic shadowing* and describes it as listening and speaking at the same time when what is spoken is the same as what is listened to. She says it is a paced auditory task, which involves the immediate vocalization of auditorily presented stimuli, i.e., a word-for-word repetition in the same language, parrot-style of a message presented through headphones. This kind of repetition means that each syllable is repeated as soon as it is heard. The process of immediate repetition tends to rely primarily on working memory. Because the limits of working memory are so brief, people cannot usually remember the messages on which they have practiced immediate repetition because there is not enough time to process the message into meaningful units.

The Role of Immediate Repetition in the Interpretation Process

Immediate repetition in one's L1 is routinely used at the preinterpreting or the admission stage as a screening technique in order to determine if the prospective interpreter can listen and speak simultaneously. deGroot's (1997) analysis of recent research suggests that the skill of immediate repetition shares many components with simultaneous interpretation. deGroot points out that the process of immediate repetition and the process of simultaneous interpretation both require comprehending and producing speech simultaneously and also speech that was not originally that of the repeater or the interpreter.

Being able to listen and speak is an essential skill in the interpreting process. Lambert indicates four categories into which these performances tend to fall: (1) people who find listening and speaking at the same time effortless, (2) people who can repeat the beginning of a sentence, but can't complete the repetition properly, (3) people who use the pauses in the text as a time for the repetition, and (4) people who are totally incoherent but keep talking. Ideally, with practice, immediate repetition can become effortless. When immediate repetition becomes effortless, then one more aspect of simultaneity is controlled by the interpreter's cognitive processing ability.

When a cognitive process such as this one becomes more effortless, more of the interpreter's cognitive processing can be devoted to other aspects of the interpretation process.

There are at least seven other reasons why immediate repetition is a valuable and interesting tool for interpreters. Here are some of the things that the ability to use immediate repetition can tell us.

1. The interpreter is not distracted by his or her own voice during the process.
2. There is an ability to manage this aspect of simultaneity.
3. There is an ability to simultaneously perform a synthesis and segmentation of discourse elements. This means that the interpreter can grasp the larger meaning of the message while still being able to break the message down into smaller parts for processing.
4. There is an ability to reformulate the text (Kurz, 1992). This means that the interpreter is able to listen and to create the text again in spoken form.
5. There may be an ability to monitor accuracy of output. With practice, the ability to check for accuracy usually improves.
6. There may be an ability to monitor distance behind the source.
7. Interference can be attended to or filtered out.

There are real-world professional uses for immediate repetition. For example, when two interpreters work together as a team, one serves as the back-up interpreter. The back-up interpreter can sometimes provide missing words or sentences to the interpreter who is speaking, if the working interpreter has missed part of the message. In this case the working interpreter listens to the back-up interpreter and simply repeats the information provided by the back-up interpreter. Then the working interpreter goes on with the interpretation process. The information from the back-up interpreter may seem like interference. Interference means that an additional distraction occurs during the interpretation process. In order for the interpretation to continue, the information provided by the back-up interpreter must be attended to quickly and accurately, rather than filtered out or ignored. In the case of American Sign Language to English interpretation, this requires the intake of ongoing visual information from the signer and incoming and possibly unexpected auditory information from the back-up interpreter.

Immediate Repetition Exercises

EXERCISE 4.1

Introduction

DAVID BURNIGHT

Directions

It will take approximately one minute to do the repetition. After repeating, answer the study questions and do the follow-up exercise. You will need a quiet place to work where you will not be interrupted and where you can record your responses to this selection. Find this selection on your DVD.

You will need to record yourself while you are engaged in immediate repetition. Have your recorder ready and press the record button. Then turn on the DVD player and pause it so that you can take a moment to look at the speaker before you begin. Play the selection on the DVD and begin repeating as soon as the selection starts. After you have finished repeating this short exercise, turn off the recorder and answer the study questions. Remember during this exercise that you are not required to remember what you repeat.

Study Questions

1. Listen to the recording of your voice while you were repeating. Is your spoken English understandable? Close your eyes and listen to your speech, can you understand yourself easily? Could someone else understand your recording easily? Does your recording match the speaker's message? Do your intonation patterns match those of the speaker?

____

____

____

____

____

2. Read the transcript while listening to your recording. Circle any areas in the transcript where your repetitions either do not match what the speaker said or are unintelligible.

3. Did your own voice distract you or prevent you from listening to the speaker? What strategy can you develop to overcome this distraction?

4. Did listening to the speaker interfere with your ability to repeat? What strategy can you develop to overcome this distraction?

5. Repeat the exercise and see if your spoken English is more understandable the second time. Do the intonation patterns of your repetition better match the speaker's?

Transcript for *Introduction,* David Burnight

My name is David Burnight. I have been a campus minister at San Diego State University for many years, now retired. I grew up in southern California. I've been a carpenter, a Navy officer, but most of my life I spent being a university pastor on the university campus.

Five-Step Follow-up

Step 1 **Observation**

Review your answers to the study questions.

Step 2 **Selection**

Select the portions of your performance that you circled in Study Question 2. These should be the areas that you circled as needing improvement.

Step 3 **Analysis**

With regard to the areas you selected as needing improvement, which provided more interference or greater distraction while you were repeating, your voice or the speaker's voice?

Step 4 **Assessment**

Did your spoken English match the wording of the speaker's message?

Did your spoken English convey the same message as the speaker's?

Step 5 **Action**

Develop a plan for action based on your analysis and assessment. For example, do you need to concentrate more on your own voice or that of the speaker in order to be able to repeat? Practice immediate repetition using other prerecorded material and record your voice while repeating. Note that it is not necessary to remember what you repeated, but only that you repeated accurately for as long as the speaker continues.

EXERCISE 4.2

The Scare

JEFF HARDISON

Directions

It will take approximately two and a half minutes to do the exercise. After completing the repetition answer the study questions and do the follow-up. You will need a quiet place to work where you will not be interrupted and where you can record your responses to this selection. Find this selection on your DVD. You will need to record yourself while you are engaged in immediate repetition. Have your recorder ready and press the record button. Then turn on the DVD player and pause it so that you can take a moment to look at the speaker before you begin. Play the selection on the DVD and begin repeating as soon as the selection starts. After you have finished repeating this exercise, turn off the recorder and answer the study questions. Remember, during this exercise you are not required to remember what you repeat.

Study Questions

1. Listen to the recording of your voice while you were repeating. Is your spoken English understandable? Close your eyes and listen to your speech; can you understand yourself easily? Could someone else understand your recording easily? Does your recording match the speaker's message? Do your intonation patterns match those of the speaker?

 ____

 ____

 ____

 ____

2. Listen to the recording of your voice while you were repeating. Is your spoken English understandable? Does it match the speaker's message? Do your intonation patterns match those of the speaker?

 ____

 ____

 ____

 ____

 ____

3. Read the transcript while listening to your recording. Circle any areas in the transcript where your repetitions either do not match what the speaker said or are unintelligible.

 ____

 ____

4. Did your own voice distract you or prevent you from listening to the speaker? What strategy can you develop to overcome this distraction?

5. Did listening to the speaker interfere with your ability to repeat? What strategy can you develop to overcome this distraction?

6. Repeat the exercise and see if your spoken English is more understandable the second time. Do the intonation patterns of your repetition better match the speaker's?

Transcript for *The Scare*, Jeff Hardison

Hi. My name is Jeff Hardison and I though I'd talk a little bit about some of the interesting times I had growing up in the family that I did. Real briefly, my family came from Cuba and so I spent a lot of my time growing up in the household of my grandparents and that's how I ended growing up as Cuban as I did.

Um, my grandparents' daughter, their youngest daughter my aunt Griselle and I used to hang out a lot together. But I was kind of like the little brother who always was tagging along and she would get annoyed with that. But she found interesting ways to remind me that sometimes I might not want to do that. And there was this one time I can remember when she was going to stay up late with some friends of hers to watch a horror movie. And ah, this particular horror movie was a werewolf movie. And I just pleaded and pleaded until finally she gave in and let me watch it with her and her friends; she was having a sleepover at the time. Well, when the movie was over, I went, ah went to sleep. And of course, you know, I was a little kid at the time, I wasn't much older than eight. And, ah so I fell asleep. I was probably a bit scared at the time. Well my aunt had this big bear, teddy bear that her boyfriend had won for her in a carnival. It must have been about yay big; I would say maybe four feet, four and half feet. And what she did is she waited until I was good and asleep and then got the bear, put it nose to nose with me and then woke me up. Well, of course I screamed bloody murder. Um about this time my grandmother came running in. And you have to picture, my grandmother is about four feet tall. She was just a tiny little woman. And she was so mad at my aunt, she like pulled off her sandals and started chasing her around the house. It was the funniest thing I'd ever seen. Actually, it was almost worth it to see that last piece happen.

Five-Step Follow-up

Step 1 Observation

Review your answers to the study questions.

Step 2 **Selection**

Select the portions of your performance that you circled in Study Question 2. These should be the areas that you circled as being different in content than the original.

Step 3 **Analysis**

In the areas that you selected in step 2 as needing improvement, which provided the greater interference, your voice or the speaker's voice? Did you notice any attempts to repair errors? What happened if you lost your place?

If you recorded yourself while repeating, look at that recording and see if you notice any nonverbal behaviors, such as rocking, leg swinging, or grimacing while repeating?

____

____

____

____

Step 4 **Assessment**

Did your spoken English match the wording of the speaker's message?

Did your spoken English convey the same message as the speaker's? If there is evidence that the message is skewed in your repetition, try to determine if it is due to errors at the word level or if it is due to errors in intonation patterns.

____

____

____

____

Step 5 **Action**

Develop a plan for action based on your analysis and assessment. For example, action plans can include practicing immediate repetition on other spoken English material and audiotaping your work. In that additional practice, see if you need to concentrate more on your own voice or that of the speaker in order to be able to repeat. Note that it is not necessary to remember what you repeated, but only that you repeated accurately for as long as the speaker continues. If you can record yourself, examine your performance for nonverbal movements. Repeat the same selection until you have eliminated those movements or visual distractions. If your work included comments from you about your performance, repeat the selection and work to eliminate those comments to yourself.

____

____

____

____

EXERCISE 4.3

The Cake

PAM CRISOSTOMO

Directions

It will take approximately five minutes to do the exercise. After completing the exercise answer the study questions and do the follow-up. You will need a quiet place to work where you will not be interrupted and where you can record your responses to this selection. Find this selection on your DVD. You will need to record yourself while you are engaged in immediate repetition. Have your recorder ready and press the record button. Then turn on the DVD player and pause it so that you can take a moment to look at the speaker before you begin. Play the selection on the DVD and begin repeating as soon as the selection starts. After you have finished repeating this exercise, turn off the recorder and answer the study questions. Remember, during this exercise you are not required to remember what you repeat.

Study Questions

1. Listen to the recording of your voice while you were repeating. Is your spoken English understandable? Close your eyes and listen to your speech, can you understand yourself easily? Could someone else understand your recording easily?

____

____

____

____

2. Does your recording match the speaker's message? Do your intonation patterns match those of the speaker?

____

____

____

____

3. Did your own voice distract you or prevent you from listening to the speaker? What strategy can you develop to overcome this distraction?

____

____

____

____

4. Did listening to the speaker interfere with your ability to repeat? What strategy can you develop to overcome this distraction?

____

____

____

____

5. Repeat the exercise and see if your spoken English is more understandable the second time. Do the intonation patterns of your repetition better match the speaker's?

Transcript for *The Cake*, Pam Crisostomo

My name is Pam Crisostomo and I'm going to share a personal experience that I've had. I'm the oldest of four children and I'm 19 years old. And I have a sister whose name is Phyllis and she's 13 and my sister's—next sister's name is Patty, and she's 12 and I have a little brother whose name is Noel and he's 8, and so there's ten and a half years between me and Noel. Um, I was an only child for a very long time, and I was supposed to be an only child until I remember one Christmas where I asked my mother, um, well I told my mother that instead of asking Santa for toys this Christmas, I wanted a baby sister instead. So a couple of months later I had a baby sister; her name was Phyllis and so she was born in April. And in June of 1984 we were preparing for a big baptismal party for Phyllis and she was gonna get baptized at St. Charles Church; and we were gonna have a lot of visitors over—probably about, I dunno maybe over, about maybe 300 visitors. And in the process my mom had a friend whose husband made cakes. And so my mom's friend's husband made a cake that was, um, about 20 x 30—so it was a huge cake, it was decorated really nicely and there was a stork on it and there was a baby—baby in the stork—in the stork's beak, and I just remember how great a cake it was. And so my mom, um, wanted to hide the cake so like the visitors who were going to spend the night, um, coming later that evening wouldn't see the cake—kind of so she would keep it as a surprise for everybody else. And so she and her friend put the cake in a big box and then we put it in our study. Um, so later that evening my sister Phyllis' godmother came and along with her godmother she brought her husband and her two girls. And I was excited because, I mean I was pretty much a very lonely child and so having playmates was like a big deal for me and I was really excited that I had a new sister named Phyllis who was born. And so one of the girls, her name was Lisa and she was my age and her sister Rena, um, was younger—was a year younger than both of—both of us.

So we decided that we'd play a game of hide and seek. So we were playing hide and seek and we were laughing, we were having fun, I mean as all little kids do, and at one point Lisa was "it" and Rena and I hid—hid, like in the living room and we were found very easily, and so I guess after 3 or 4 rounds Lisa—it was Lisa's turn to be "it" and so Lisa was "it". And it just wasn't working right; we were having fun, we were having a lot of fun but people were finding each other too easily. So I took Lisa—Lisa and I hid in the study room 'cause I figured that would be the best place to hide. And so Lisa and I went to the study and we ran really quickly and I remember the door slamming really loud and it was a wonder that Rena didn't find us just by the sound of the door slamming. And so we were really tired. I remember, like, laughing really hard. And Lisa decided to sit down. And Lisa sat down on the box that had the cake in it. And it was horrendous. Um, I screamed 'cause the box that she had sat on had the cake in it and so part of the cake was ruined. So I screamed and I called my mom and all I remember was I got spanked. I was six years old and I got spanked, whereas Lisa and Rena didn't get in trouble at all, but, um, my mom said that it was my fault because this was my house and we weren't supposed to be in the study anyway. And the cake was ruined—this big, beautiful cake was ruined.

So, I kinda thought, when I was, y'know, little I thought that was kind of an injustice for me because it wasn't my fault. All I did was go and play hide and seek and I remember my dad telling the visitors the next day when the cake was out, um, about how the kids were playing and that's why half of the cake was ruined. But that's something I'm never gonna forget, kind of like one of my injustices. But I look back now and I laugh, and I'm sure my mom laughs too.

Five-Step Follow-up

Step 1 Observation

Review your answers to the study questions.

Step 2 Selection

Select the portions of your performance that you circled in Study Question 2. These circles indicate places where your words did not match those of the speaker.

Step 3 Analysis

In the areas that you selected in step 2 as needing improvement, which provided the greater interference, your voice or the speaker's voice? Did you notice any attempts to repair errors? What happened if you lost your place? If you recorded yourself while repeating, look at that recording and see if you notice any nonverbal behaviors, such as rocking, leg swinging, or grimacing while repeating?

Step 4 Assessment

Did your spoken English match the wording of the speaker's spoken English? Did your spoken English convey the same message as the speaker's? If there is evidence that the message is skewed in your repetition, try to determine if it is due to errors at the word level or if it is due to errors in intonation patterns.

____

____

____

____

Step 5 **Action**

Develop a plan for action based on your analysis and assessment. For example, action plans can include practicing immediate repetition on other spoken English material and audiotaping your work. In that additional practice, see if you need to concentrate more on your own voice or that of the speaker in order to be able to repeat. Note that it is not necessary to remember what you repeated, but only that you repeated accurately for as long as the speaker continues. If you can record yourself, examine your performance for nonverbal movements. Repeat the same selection until you have eliminated those movements or visual distractions. If your work included comments from you about your performance, repeat the selection and work to eliminate those comments to yourself.

____

____

____

____

Progress Tracking Sheet

This sheet is designed to help you keep track of which exercises you have completed and how well you have done on these exercises. See page 12 for a full description of how to use the Progress Tracking Sheet.

Exercise Number	Date	First Performance	Study Questions	Follow-up Activity	Questions and Reminders	Date	Second Performance
Exercise 4.1 Quantitative							
Qualitative							
Exercise 4.2 Quantitative							
Qualitative							
Exercise 4.3 Quantitative							
Qualitative							
Quantitative Totals							

UNIT 5

Delayed Repetition

Introduction

After immediate repetition skills are in place it is important to add the skill of delayed repetition. Delayed repetition means repetition that begins after an enforced waiting period. That waiting period could be a very brief time interval, or it could be an interval based on a unit of information such as a phrase (Lambert, 1989). By adding a delay to the repetition process, the foundations for gaining control of decalage, processing time, or lag time can be enhanced. Decalage, processing time, lag time, and ear–voice span all refer to the same thing. These words refer to the amount of time that elapses between the moment that the interpreter hears the message and the moment that the interpreter renders the interpretation of that message.

The ability to perform delayed repetition at the phrase level indicates the ability to segment incoming messages into component parts or phrases. Delayed-repetition ability forms the basis for developing processing time during simultaneous interpretation. It is important to be able to find the natural breaks in spoken English in order to be able to effectively use processing time while interpreting.

Delayed repetition requires the use of both long-term memory and working memory or short-term memory, although it is necessary to hear an entire meaning unit before continuing with the repetition, rather than a single word. In general, more effort will be required for delayed repetition than immediate repetition. This is especially true if the listener is not familiar with the procedures or propositions in the text. The ability to successfully manage delayed repetition indicates the ability to effectively use the following: listening, finding phrases, monitoring phrasal distance, speaking while listening, and monitoring output of the repetition. All of these abilities are important components of the interpretation process.

The Role of Delayed Repetition in the Interpretation Process

The ability to use processing time effectively is an essential and important part of the interpretation process. The ability to listen and repeat with a delay is one aspect of training in simultaneous interpretation. Ingram (1984) described processing time this way. "To lag, or in simultaneous interpreting, it refers to the span of time between the interpreter's perception of the source language and the subsequent production of the target language rendition. It is the period of time between the interpreter's input and output." Interpreters with greater control of decalage skills tend to make fewer errors (Lambert, 1989, p. 49).

Another author, Cokely (1986), studied four interpreters to analyze the effect of processing time on number of errors or miscues during the interpretation. He found that interpreters who could use the longest amount of processing time tended to make fewer errors. He analyzed various types of errors. The types of errors he studied were omissions, additions, substitutions, intrusions, and anomalies. When all types of errors were grouped, the interpreters in the Cokely study who used a two-second processing time made more than twice as many errors as those who used a four-second processing time. Those who used a four-second processing time made twice as many errors as those who used a six-second processing time. Cokely summarizes the results of his study by saying "The greater lag time, the more information available; the more information available, the greater the level of comprehension" (1986, p. 67).

The importance of being able to use processing time well in the interpretation process cannot be overstated. Delayed repetition in the interpreter's L1 is likely to be a building block for developing processing time during the interpretation process.

Delayed Repetition Exercises

EXERCISE 5.1

My Trip to Costa Rica

AMBER LEWNES

Directions

It will take approximately three minutes to do the exercise. After completing the exercise answer the study questions and do the follow-up exercise. You will need a quiet place to work where you will not be interrupted and where you can record your responses to this selection. Note the title of the speech to help prepare you for the possible content of the speech. Find this selection on your DVD.

You will need to record yourself while you are engaged in delayed repetition. Have your recorder ready and press the record button. Then turn on the DVD player and pause it so that you can take a moment to look at the speaker before you begin. Play the selection on the DVD and begin repeating as soon as you hear the beep. Maintain this distance behind the speaker throughout this exercise. After you have finished repeating this exercise, turn off your recorder and answer the study questions. Remember, during this exercise you are not required to remember what you repeat.

Study Questions

1. Listen to the recording of your voice. Is your repetition approximately four seconds or an idea unit or phrase, after the speaker's utterance during the entire selection? Is this kind of repetition more difficult than immediate repetition? Why or why not?

____

____

____

____

____

2. Did your own voice distract you or prevent you from listening to the speaker? Did listening to the speaker interfere with your ability to repeat? Explain.

3. Is your spoken English intelligible? Do your words match the speaker's? Does your message match the speaker's? Refer to the transcript and circle any portions where the message you repeated does not match the source message.

4. Do variations in your intonation patterns affect the meaning? How? Did you make any comments that the speaker did not make? If so, how does that affect the message?

5. Mark the places on your transcript where you were not able to maintain a four-second or phrase distance behind the speaker. If you lost your place during the repetition process, what caused that and how did you find your place again? Do you "chunk" the information to repeat or do you keep a steady flow? Which works better for you?

Transcript for *My Trip to Costa Rica,* Amber Lewnes

My name is Amber Lewnes and I'm gonna tell you about my trip to Costa Rica [beep] that I took when I was 16 years old. I flew down to go visit a friend of mine that had lived next door to me (she's my best friend) for years and she moved down to Costa Rica and I went to go see her after 3 years and I flew down on a plane by myself, which was kind of nerve-wracking at 16.

And when I went there I learned all sorts of things—like different culture—the whole different culture, different new words in Spanish, um... The most interesting thing that I learned, or that I found in Costa Rica was, um, when we went to a Catholic church. It was a old cathedral that had been built in the 1700s, I think. And um, it was a tradition that any time one of the patrons of the church had lost something close to them, like anything from a leg to a family member, they'd make a symbol of it in a gold or silver charm. And they'd hang this charm in the basement of the church. And there was just rows and rows of little charms all over the place of different things that people had lost. As kind of a remembrance to what we don't have anymore and to keep in mind the things that we do have and to appreciate them. And I found that really fascinating.

And I think the trip was a good experience—I got to see the rainforest before it's cut down any more and I got to meet a lot of interesting people and learn a lot of things that I could not have done so in this country. And that was my trip to Costa Rica.

Five-Step Follow-up

Step 1 Observation

Review your answers to the study questions.

Step 2 Selection

Select the portions of your performance that you circled in Study Question 3. These circles indicate places where your words did not match those of the speaker.

Step 3 Analysis

In the area that you selected in step 2 as needing improvement, which provided the greater interference, your voice or the speaker's voice? Did you notice any nonverbal behaviors on your part, such as rocking, leg swinging, or grimacing while repeating? If you repaired content errors, analyze the repair to see if the repair corrected the error. Describe what happened if you lost your place.

Step 4 Assessment

Does your spoken English convey the same words as the speaker's? Does your spoken English convey the same message as the speaker's? If there is evidence that the message is skewed in your repetition, try to determine if it is due to errors in the repetition of the words, use of processing time, errors in intonation patterns, or in phrase construction.

Step 5 Action

Develop a plan for action based on your analysis and assessment. For example, action plans can include practicing immediate repetition on other spoken English material and audiotaping your work. In that additional practice, see if you need to concentrate more on your own voice or that of the speaker in order to be able to repeat. Note that it is not necessary to remember what you repeated, but only that you repeated accurately for as long as the speaker continues. If you can record yourself, examine your performance for nonverbal movements. Repeat the same selection until you have eliminated those movements or visual distractions. If your work included comments from you about your performance, repeat the selection and work to eliminate those comments to yourself.

EXERCISE 5.2

How to Tie a Bow

LORRAINE OLDHAM

Directions

It will take approximately three minutes to do the exercise. After completing the exercise answer the study questions and do the follow-up exercises. You will need a quiet place to work where you will not be interrupted and where you can record your responses to this selection. Note the title of the speech to help prepare you for the possible content of the speech. Find this selection on your DVD.

You will need to record yourself while you are engaged in delayed repetition. Have your recorder ready and press the record button. Then turn on the DVD player and pause it so that you can take time to look at the speaker before you begin. Play the selection on the DVD and begin repeating as soon as you hear the beep tone. Maintain this four-second distance behind the speaker throughout the exercise. After you have finished repeating this exercise, turn off your recorder and answer the study questions. Remember, during this exercise you are not required to remember what you repeat.

Study Questions

1. Listen to the recording of your voice. Is your repetition approximately four seconds, or an idea unit or phrase, after the speaker's utterance during the entire selection? Is this kind of repetition more difficult than immediate repetition? Why or why not?

____

____

____

____

2. Did your own voice distract you or prevent you from listening to the

speaker? Did listening to the speaker interfere with your ability to repeat? Explain.

____

____

____

____

____

3. Is your spoken English intelligible? Do your words match the speaker's? Does your message match the speaker's? Refer to the transcript and circle any portions where the message you repeated does not match the source message.

____

____

____

____

____

4. Do variations in your intonation patterns affect the meaning? How? Did you make any comments that the speaker did not make? If so, how does that affect the message?

____

____

____

5. Mark the places on your transcript where you were not able to maintain a four-second, or phrase distance, behind the speaker. If you lost your place during the repetition process, what caused that and how did you find your place again? Do you "chunk" the information to repeat or do

you keep a steady flow? Which works better for you?

Transcript for *How to Tie a Bow,* Lorraine Oldham

Hi. I'm Lorraine Oldham and I would like to be able to demonstrate to you the way I learned best how to make a bow for gift-wrap [beep]. And I would recommend, first of all, getting a wide ribbon and a satin finish and it really makes it a lot easier to work with. What I'd like to do is just cut the ribbon about, uh, just long enough to loop it over and then pinch it together. And at each loop I am going to pinch it where my fingers hold it, and that is really the key. What I do is pinch and twist, and in the twisting process I loop again, and then twist again, and then continue to successive loops, always twisting as I loop. Just like this. And you can make your bow as large or small—just by working the ribbon into consecutive loops. And just for demonstration purposes I will stop here for now, and just—what you want to do is make sure you have ready a tie, an already cut piece of ribbon that you can use to tie around the center and crimp the loops together this way. And it's always helpful to have extra fingers when you do this because it becomes very awkward otherwise. Sometimes it's ok to use teeth. And I just pull it tight, and as you can see, you have a nice bow for gift-wrap. And it always helps to just cut your extra pieces on an angle. And you can use these on wreaths, making them very large. You can use them on small packages, again adjusting the size of the bow just by making the loops the size that you need for the particular package or wreath that you want. And that's it. Happy wrapping!

Five-Step Follow-up

Step 1 Observation

Review your answers to the study questions.

Step 2 Selection

Select the portions of your performance that you circled in Study Question 3. These circles indicate places where your words did not match those of the speaker.

Step 3 Analysis

In the area that you selected in step 2 as needing improvement, which provided the greater interference, your voice or the speaker's voice? Did you notice any nonverbal behaviors on your part, such as rocking, leg swinging, or grimacing while repeating? If you repaired content errors, analyze them to see if the repair corrected the error. Describe what happened if you lost your place.

Step 4 Assessment

Does your spoken English convey the same words as the speaker's? Does your spoken English convey the same message as the speaker's? If there is evidence that the message is skewed in your delayed repetition, try to determine if it is due to errors in the repetition of the words, use of processing time, intonation patterns, or phrase construction.

Step 5 Action

Develop a plan for action based on your analysis and assessment. For example, action plans can include practicing immediate repetition on other spoken English material and audiotaping your work. In that additional practice, see if you need to concentrate more on your own voice or that of the speaker in order to be able to repeat. Note that it is not necessary to remember what you repeated, but only that you repeated accurately for as long as the speaker continues. If you can record yourself, examine your performance for nonverbal movements. Repeat the same selection until you have eliminated those movements or visual distractions. If your work included comments from you about your performance, repeat the selection and work to eliminate those comments to yourself.

____

____

____

EXERCISE 5.3

How to Put in a Zipper

MARQUESSA BROWN

Directions

It will take approximately six minutes to do the exercise. After completing the exercise answer the study questions and do the follow-up. You will need a quiet place to work where you will not be interrupted and where you can record your responses to this selection. Note the title of the speech to help you prepare for the possible content of the speech. Find this selection on your DVD.

You will need to record yourself while you are engaged in delayed repetition. Have your recorder ready and press the record button. Then turn on the DVD player and pause it so that you can take a moment to look at the speaker before you begin. Play the selection on the DVD and begin repeating as soon as you hear the beep tone. Maintain this four-second distance behind the speaker throughout this exercise. After you have finished repeating this exercise, turn off your recorder and answer the study questions. Remember, during this exercise you are not required to remember what you repeat.

Study Questions

1. Listen to the recording of your voice. Is your repetition approximately four seconds, or an idea unit or phrase, after the speaker's utterance during the entire selection? Is this kind of repetition more difficult than immediate repetition? Why or why not?

2. Did your own voice distract you or prevent you from listening to the speaker? Did listening to the speaker interfere with your ability to repeat? Explain.

3. Is your spoken English intelligible? Do your words match the speaker's? Does your message match the speaker's? Refer to the transcript and circle any portions where the message you repeated does not match the source message.

4. Do variations in your intonation patterns affect the meaning? How? Did you make any comments that the speaker did not make? If so, how does that affect the message?

5. Mark the places on your transcript where you were not able to maintain a four-second distance behind the speaker. If you lost your place during the repetition process, what caused that and how did you find your place again? Do you "chunk" the information to repeat or do you keep a steady flow? Which works better for you?

Transcript for *How to Put in a Zipper,* Marquessa Brown

Hi. My name is Marquessa Brown. I'm going to share with you very simple instructions for putting a zipper in a dress [beep]. I believe I'll start with the assumption that everybody listening to this or looking at this isn't going to know two things. They're not going to know how to use a sewing machine, and they're not going to know how to sew. So let me start with some very simple directions about a sewing machine and how you operate it. A sewing machine has a big wheel on the right. It has a needle and um, a needle foot in the center. And it has a plate on the bottom. The plate that's on the bottom is directly over the needle, which is located in the needle foot. It also has a pedal that's on the floor. Now the object is, you have to mash the pedal with your right foot while holding the fabric with two hands so that the fabric can easily glide through the needle. And you've gotta hold it to kinda keep it from going in all kinds of directions so that your fabric won't be crooked and lines everywhere and it's sewn incorrectly. So you're going to—you don't have to worry too much about the wheel. The wheel just turns automatically. But you've gotta learn how to get the right amount of pressure on the foot—on the foot as you're guiding the fabric through. OK, so that's pretty much how the machine works.

Now, there are two ways that you can put a zipper in. You can put the zipper into your garment before you've sewn the entire garment together, or you can complete the entire garment and then put your zipper in. I think it's probably easier to put the zipper in before you've sewn the entire garment together, because you just have less fabric to work with, and I think that makes it a little bit easier when you're trying to guide the fabric through the machine and over the needle. OK.

Now I'm just gonna talk very quickly about how you do it either way. If you want to put the zipper in before you've put your entire garment together, then you want to start with the pieces that the zipper is going to fit in. So let's assume that we're making a skirt, and we're going to have the zipper in the back of the skirt. The zi—the skirt therefore is going to have an opening in the center and the zipper is going to fit directly in this center opening. So what you're going to do—and I think for new sewers it's probably best to do what we call a basting first. A basting basically means that you sew your zipper in by hand first; simply using a needle and thread just sew it up one side and you sew it up the other side. It's very important to make sure that the fabric totally covers the zipper. So often when people are—are learning to sew and putting in zippers for the first time, they tend to have the silver or the shiny part of the zipper showing in the middle. But the key when you're basting is to be sure that the left and the right cover the center of the zipper when you baste it in. OK, so let's say you've sewn up the left side, you've sewn up the right side, the zipper has—the fabric is totally covering the zipper so that you cannot see your zipper. Now, after you've done that and you've got this one piece of fabric: the back part of your dress. You're going to take it and you're going to lift up the needle. There's a little flipper on the back of your sewing machine. So you flip it up, you take your fabric, you put it under there. It's probably better to start sewing on the right side of your zipper.

So, you take your fabric, you put it under, you let down the lever, you put your foot on the pedal and you start sewing. Guiding your fabric all the time. And you want to slow—and you want to sew very slowly. So you're gonna start probably at the bottom and you're gonna sew up one side. Now, if you know anything about zippers the top part of the zipper's kinda thick. So it's going to be important when you're sewing that when you get to the top part and the needle doesn't go over the thick part of the zipper that you stop at that point. So you're gonna sew straight up until you get to that thick part of the zipper and you can't sew it any more. You stop, take the—this is when you're gonna use your wheel on the side. You take your wheel and you turn it up so that the needle comes out of your material. You take your fabric out—um—and then you move it over to the other side. So you're gonna sew again where you did your basting, and you're gonna sew that up. When you finish with that, you take it out again, you pull your zipper down, and then you're gonna sew those two places on both sides where it was too thick to sew it with the—um—zipper up. So now that you've got the zipper pulled down you can get your needle to go through on both sides. That's basically how you put a zipper in.

Five-Step Follow-up

Step 1 Observation

Review your answers to the study questions.

Step 2 Selection

Select the portions of your performance that you circled in Study Question 3. These circles indicate places where your words did not match those of the speaker.

Step 3 Analysis

In the area that you selected in step 2 as needing improvement, which provided the greater interference, your voice or the speaker's voice? Did you notice any nonverbal behaviors on your part, such as rocking, leg swinging, or grimacing while repeating? If you repaired content errors, analyze them to see if the repair corrected the error. Describe what happened if you lost your place.

____

____

____

____

Step 4 Assessment

Does your spoken English convey the same words as the speaker's? Does your spoken English convey the same message as the speaker's? If there is evidence that the message is skewed in your repetition, try to determine if it is due to errors in the repetition of the words, intonation patterns, or phrase construction.

____

____

____

____

Step 5 Action

Develop a plan for action based on your analysis and assessment. For example, action plans can include practicing immediate repetition on other spoken English material and audiotaping your work. In that additional practice, see if you need to concentrate more on your own voice or that of the speaker in order to be able to repeat. Note that it is not necessary to remember what you repeated, but only that you repeated accurately for as long as the speaker continues. If you can record yourself, examine your performance for nonverbal movements. Repeat the same selection until you have eliminated those movements or visual distractions. If your work included comments from you about your performance, repeat the selection and work to eliminate those comments to yourself.

____

____

____

Progress Tracking Sheet

This sheet is designed to help you keep track of which exercises you have completed and how well you have done on these exercises. See page 12 for a full description of how to use the Progress Tracking Sheet.

Exercise Number	Date	First Performance	Study Questions	Follow-up Activity	Questions and Reminders	Date	Second Performance
Exercise 5.1 Quantitative							
Qualitative							
Exercise 5.2 Quantitative							
Qualitative							
Exercise 5.3 Quantitative							
Qualitative							
Quantitative Totals							

UNIT 6 Number Repetition

Introduction

This unit provides an introduction to developing cognitive strategies needed for listening to speeches with numbers in spoken English and accurately remembering the numbers. Originally this process was called *digit processing*. Here, the process is called number repetition because you will not actually be processing or changing the numbers in any way. The exercises in this unit require that you correctly remember the numbers long enough to repeat them.

The Role of Number Repetition in the Interpretation Process

Practice in various kinds of repetition is one of many training techniques used in interpreter education programs. In actual interpretation, repetition is not generally used, except in certain instances where words like proper names are used and when those words do not have an equivalent in the TL. During the interpretation process, the numbers in a text are not really processed in the same way that the rest of the message is. Instead, the *names* of the numbers are transcoded into the TL. For example, the number 25 has a name. The name of that combination of characters in English is twenty-five. If an interpreter hears the English word "twenty-five" during a speech to be interpreted, the interpreter must find the exact lexical equivalent in the TL.

Numbers are not subject to aspects of cultural influence and do not need to be culturally mediated by the interpreter. In order to be accurate, the interpreter must be able to accurately remember the exact number long enough to find the name of that number in the TL.

Moser-Mercer (1983) who uses the term processing of numbers suggests that numbers are notoriously problematic for interpreters. "The processing of numbers requires the accurate preservation of exact numeral information in running discourse." She says, "From a language information processing point of view, the processing of numbers differs from that of continuous text, in that numbers are largely unpredictable" (p. 59) and require something like a sudden shifting of gears. This means that the context does not increase the interpreter's chances of correctly filling in the blank if the number is missed. Pattern inference skills are not likely to help the interpreter decide what number could fill in the blank. For example, if an interpreter hears the following sentence fragment, "The cost of the house will be ________" there is no way for the interpreter to be able to correctly fill in the blank due to the unpredictability of numbers.

Lambert (1989) points out that "Digits have meaning only when associated with words, and they are highly unpredictable" (p. 51). She suggests that the difficulty may be due to the possibility that digits are processed differently than the rest of the message, perhaps involving a switch in cerebral dominance. Gile (1995) says that numbers are likely to cause problems for interpreters, not because they require a great deal of processing capacity, but because numbers are a more "vulnerable" signal. By this Gile means that numbers are short in duration and are low in redundancy. Another way to look at Gile's idea is to realize that the name of the number does not take long to say and is usually not repeated. Gile goes on to say that the numerical information can be lost during even a brief lapse of attention. Once the number has been missed due to poor attention strategies, or forgotten due to poor memory strategies, it is quite likely that the entire interpretation process can break down at that point.

The exercises in this unit are all intralingual. That means that all the exercises are in English and you will respond in English. The numbers do not have to be interpreted, merely repeated. Being able to remember the number long enough to repeat it correctly is the first step in building skill in interpreting material that contains numbers. It is possible that, even though you may have developed immediate- and delayed-repetition skills in the previous units, you may find this unit more difficult because of the numbers in the speeches you will hear. Concentrate on correct repetition of the numbers and try to keep going in the repetition process, even if you make a mistake. First, you should practice immediate repetition, then use the beep at the four-second mark to practice delayed repetition.

Number Repetition Exercises

EXERCISE 6.1

How to Play the California Lottery

AMY BOUCK

Directions

It will take approximately two minutes to do the exercise. After completing the exercise answer the study questions and do the follow-up exercise. You will need a quiet place to work where you will not be interrupted and where you can record your responses to this selection. Note the title of the speech to help you prepare for the possible content of the speech. Find this selection on your DVD.

You will need to record yourself while you are engaged in repetition of the speeches with numbers. Have your recorder ready and press the record button. Then turn on the DVD player and pause the DVD so that you can take time to look at the speaker before you begin. Play the selection on the DVD and begin immediate repetition.

In repeating numbers, you will necessarily need a short amount of time between hearing the number and repeating it. This exercise does not require an enforced delay before repeating. Ideally, you will do this exercise twice. The first time without a delay and the second time with a delay. The DVD has a beep tone to mark the four-second point that you can use as a cue to begin delayed repetition. Concentrate on accurate repetition of each number you hear. After you have finished repeating this exercise, turn off your recorder and answer the study questions. Remember, during this exercise you are not required to remember the content of what you repeated.

Study Questions

1. Listen to the recording of your voice. Was repetition of a speech with numbers more difficult than immediate or delayed repetition? Why or why not?

____

____

2. Did you make any comments that the speaker did not make? If you did, how did those additions affect the message?

3. Was your spoken English intelligible? Did your words match the speaker's? Did your message match the speaker's? Were you able to maintain uniform control of the volume of your voice during the exercise?

4. Did errors in repeating any of the numbers affect the meaning? How?

5. Listen to the recording of yourself while reading the transcript. Circle the places on the transcript where you were not able to correctly repeat the numbers. If you lost your place during the repetition process, what caused that and how did you find your place again? Repeat the exercise and see if your ability to repeat the numbers correctly is improved when you are more familiar with the material.

____

____

____

____

____

Transcript for *How to Play the California Lottery,* Amy Bouck

Hi. My name is Amy Bouck, and I'm gonna give you directions on how to play the lottery [beep]. First you have to pick six numbers, uh, these can be numbers that are your favorite numbers, your lucky numbers, uh, numbers of ages of people in your family or any other random numbers you feel you ought to choose. Once you've chosen these six numbers, you go up to your local convenience store, where they have a lottery station. You go over to the station and pick up the piece of paper that has the name "Sup—Super Lotto" on the top. Uh, once you pick one of these papers you'll notice that it has a lot of numbers on it with bubbles around the numbers. You fill in with a pen the numbers that you have chosen. Uh, the numbers I normally choose are: 4, 20, 24, 36, 47 and 50. All the numbers have to be between 1 and 51. Once you've filled in all the numbers on the sheet that you wish to choose you take that form and $1.00 over to the cashier. The cashier takes your form and puts it through a machine, which spits out a formal ticket. This has all six of your numbers on it. Once you have your ticket you then go home and wait for them to draw your numbers—hopefully they're your numbers. And that's how you play the lottery.

Five-Step Follow-up

Step 1 Observation

Review your answers to the study questions.

Step 2 Selection

Refer to your answers to Study Question 5 where you circled the places where the number repetition was inaccurate. For each circle, determine the effect of the error on the message. Was it serious or not serious?

Step 3 Analysis

Analyze the answers used in step 2 more closely. Note how many numbers were omitted. Note if another number was substituted for the correct number. In cases where you substituted a number, was the substitution close to the original number in ordinal sequence?

Step 4 Assessment

What effect did errors in number repetition have on the meaning of the overall message? If the volume of your voice dropped off during number repetition, how did that affect the message? Was the rest of your repetition accurate, apart from the number repetition? Assess your work and determine if errors in repetition of the message followed errors in number repetition.

Step 5 **Action**

Develop a plan for action based on your analysis and assessment. For example, practice number repetition until you have found a way to repeat accurately. Incorporate the repetition strategies from immediate repetition to help you do this. If your performance included nonverbal movements, work to eliminate those in future practice. If your work included comments from you about your work, eliminate those comments in future practice. Practice this exercise again and instead of immediate repetition use delayed repetition.

EXERCISE 6.2

How to Play Blackjack

ED PERKIN

Directions

It will take approximately nine minutes to do the exercise. After completing the exercise, answer the study questions and do the follow-up exercise. You will need a quiet place to work where you will not be interrupted and where you can record your responses to this selection. Note the title of the speech to help you prepare for the possible content of the speech. Find this selection on your DVD.

You will need to record yourself while you are engaged in repetition of the speeches with numbers. Have your recorder ready and press the record button. Then turn on the DVD player and pause it so that you can take time to look at the speaker before you begin. Play the selection on the DVD and begin repeating as soon as the speaker has completed the first few words; you do not need to maintain a full phrase distance behind the speaker.

In repeating numbers, you will necessarily need a short amount of time between hearing the number and repeating it. Ideally, you will do this exercise twice. The first time without a delay and the second time with a delay. The DVD has a beep tone to mark the four-second point that can be used as a cue to begin delayed repetition. Concentrate on accurate repetition of each number you hear. After you have finished repeating this exercise, turn off your recorder and answer the study questions. Remember, during this exercise you are not required to remember the content of what you repeated.

Study Questions

1. Listen to the recording of your voice. Was repetition of a speech with numbers more difficult than immediate or delayed repetition? Why or why not?

   ____

   ____

   ____

2. Did you make any comments that the speaker did not make? If you did, how did those additions affect the message?

   ____

   ____

   ____

3. Was your spoken English intelligible? Did your words match the speaker's? Did your message match the speaker's? Were you able to maintain uniform control over the volume of your voice during the exercise?

   ____

   ____

4. Did errors in repeating any of the numbers affect the meaning? How?

____

____

5. Listen to the recording of yourself while reading the transcript. Circle the places on the transcript where you were not able to correctly repeat the numbers. If you lost your place during the repetition process, what caused that and how did you find your place again? Repeat the exercise and see if your ability to repeat the numbers correctly is improved when you are more familiar with the material.

____

____

Transcript for *How to Play Blackjack*, Ed Perkin

My name is Ed Perkin and I am going to discuss the game of blackjack [beep], which is, uh, a casino game played, uh, all around the world. It's also known as "pontoon" and "21." Uh, it's, uh, Las Vegas' second-biggest game after only craps, and it's also played in Atlantic City, to name a couple of the, uh, more popular places in the States where it is played. It's also played throughout the Caribbean and in the, um, Asian Pacific, um, as well as in Europe. So it's a very popular game and, um, it has become more popular recently with the advent of card counting, which is something I'm familiar with. My friends and I go to Las Vegas a couple of times a year, where we attempt to beat the casinos by counting cards.

Uh, the game—well, card-counting in particular became popular, oh, probably 30 or 40 years ago. Uh, it started with a group of scientists in the military who enjoyed playing blackjack in their spare time for fun, and after a time they realized that there was a definite strategy that should be implemented, uh, for a given playing situation. And they worked on it, and they didn't really have computers because this is going back to the '50s or so, and, uh, they didn't have any, uh, anything other than, uh, pen and paper and uh, trial and error to help 'em out. So they began to play thousands and thousands of scenarios, taking into account every mathematical consideration they could, and over time they were able to develop what is known today as the basic strategy. The basic strategy, simply, is the correct way to play a given hand in the game of blackjack.

Uh, a little background on blackjack: it's, uh, also known as "21" because the object of the game is to get, uh, to a card total of 21. You start with two cards against the dealer's two cards, and the, uh, cards are valued at their face value with the exception of face cards, which are valued at 10, and the ace, which is valued at either 1 or 11 at the player's discretion. And, uh, so for example, an ace and a 10 would equal 21 and that would be a natural winning hand. Uh, otherwise if you have some lesser total (say a 10 and 6) that would be 16. It is the player's option to take another card or to stand with what he or she has. The dealer is bound by the rule that he or she must hit anything below—at sixteen or below and stand at 17 or above. Because the player has to go first he's at a substantial disadvantage because, uh, in the cases where both bust, the dealer still takes your money. So in order to account for this substantial discrepancy, the, uh, player is given a couple of advan—advantages. Uh, one, he is paid 3 to 2 on a natural blackjack. Uh, he's allowed to "double-down": if he likes his first two cards he may double his bet and take exactly one more card, or he may "split" his two cards. Uh, and the, uh, the idea of card counting, uh, basically is that blackjack is the one game where the odds are constantly fluctuating.

Games like craps and roulette and slot machines, the odds are set. You can play and you might win in the short run, but the, uh, the odds are determined and over the long run the casino has an exact mathematical advantage which, they will, uh, win. The—blackjack, however, uh, it's completely up to the player—how good they are. Uh, if a player plays the cards correctly they can cut the casino's edge. By applying simply basic strategy, they can cut it all the way down to less than 1%. Um, however, a poor player might be givin' the casino 9 or 10% of their money, and, of course this means their bank account is wiped out pretty quickly. So it really comes down to how good the player is. Now, no matter how good you are you're never gonna get an advantage over the casino. You'll get it down into the tenths of a percent, but that's still—the casino still has the advantage over you at that point. So the only way to gain an advantage over the casino is to implement card counting.

Basically, what card counting is, is it's a way of identifying the situations where the player has an advantage over the dealer. Uh, the way this is done is in the most simple card counting methods, tens are tracked by the player. When a higher proportion of tens remain in the deck that is left to play—to be played, this favors the player. When a lower percentage of tens is left, this favors the dealer. And so you vary your bets according to how advantageous the remaining deck is. If there are a lot of tens left, you bet more. If there are a few tens, you bet the minimum or take a break and leave the casino. Uh, basically the most, uh, simple, uh, count system is what's called a point count, where the cards are valued. Now this is separate from the game—the game has the, uh, card values which I've already talked about.

Now the card counting values are as follows: using the high up one system which is the system I choose to use 3s, 4s, 5s, and 6s are valued at plus 1, while all tens, jacks, queens and kings are valued at minus 1. As you see each card fall as it's played from the deck you add or subtract from the count, starting at zero. So if you saw a five and then a six those are both valued at plus one. So plus one, plus one again's plus two. And if you saw a king that would be minus one, so you'd go back to plus one, a queen you'd be back to zero, a jack you'd be to negative one and so on. The higher the positive, the better the situation because you're removing small cards and that's leaving the tens left in the deck, which favors you.

So, for example, if you've played the first hand of a deck and the count's at plus three this is a strong situation and you should bet a higher amount than you normally would. Uh, there are three advantages that card counting gives you. One is which I've already discussed that it tells you when the count—when the deck favors you and you can bet more or less accordingly. Also, it tells you when to take "insurance." Insurance is simply a bet that the dealer will have a ten underneath their ace. It's falsely labeled insurance by the casinos in order to trick you into taking it when you shouldn't. Most dealers tell you to take insurance on a blackjack, but this is not true. In fact, because you, uh, have a ten in your hand it's actually less, uh, uh, of a situation when you should take insurance than if you had, say, a 5 and a 6, where more tens were remaining. But I digress. Uh, basically, the higher the count, the better the insurance bet. So if you—regardless of what you're holding in your hand, if you have a high count you should take insurance. Plus two or above you should take insurance. The higher—the more you should take it.

And then, the third thing that card counting will do for you is it will allow you to vary your playing strategy away from the basic strategy, which you've already learned by picking up a book in your local bookstore. Pretty much any book will have the basic strategy in it, even in a casino gift shop they'll tell you the basic strategy, which cuts your odds down to, as I said, less than 1% against you. So the casino's willing to tell you how to beat them. You've just gotta be willing to spend a couple bucks to buy one of their books. Uh, the third reason, as I said, is it allows you to vary from this basic strategy by implementing the count. For example, when you have a sixteen against a ten, basic strategy tells you to hit that hand. You should hit a sixteen against the dealer's ten.

However, it is a very marginal advantage to hit versus standing. If the count is very high, then you would actually want to stand rather than hit. So an advanced player can employ the count in order to vary their strategy and to win a whole bunch of money against the casino, which I hope that all of you out there will do.

Five-Step Follow-up

Step 1 Observation

Review your answers to the study questions.

Step 2 Selection

Refer to your answers to Study Question 5 where you circled the places where the number repetition was inaccurate. For each circle, determine the effect of the error on the message. Was it serious or not serious?

Step 3 Analysis

Analyze your answer to step 2 more closely. Note how many numbers were omitted. Note if another number was substituted for the correct number. In cases where you substituted a number, was the substitution close to the original number in ordinal sequence?

Step 4 **Assessment**

What effect did errors in number repetition have on the meaning of the overall message? If the volume of your voice dropped off during number repetition, how did that affect the message? Was the rest of your repetition accurate, apart from the number repetition? Assess your work and determine if errors in repetition of the message followed errors in number repetition.

Step 5 **Action**

Develop a plan for action based on your analysis and assessment. For example, practice number repetition until you find a way to repeat accurately. Incorporate the repetition strategies from immediate repetition to help you do this. If your performance included nonverbal movements, work to eliminate those in future practice. If your work included comments from you about your work, eliminate those comments in future practice. Practice this exercise again, and instead of immediate repetition use delayed repetition.

EXERCISE 6.3

How to Make a DNA Plasmid

PAM CRISOSTOMO

Directions

It will take approximately nine minutes to do the exercise. After completing the exercise answer the study questions and do the follow-up exercises. You will need a quiet place to work where you will not be interrupted and where you can record your responses to this selection. Note the title of the speech to help prepare you for the possible content of the speech. Find this selection on your DVD.

You will need to record yourself while you are engaged in repetition of this speech with numbers. Have your recorder ready and press the record button. Then turn on the DVD player and pause the DVD so that you can take time to look at the speaker before you begin. Play the selection on the DVD and begin repeating as soon as the speaker begins. You do not need to maintain a full phrase distance behind the speaker.

In repeating numbers, you will necessarily need a short amount of time between hearing the number and repeating it. Ideally, you will do this exercise twice. The first time without a delay and the second time with a delay. The DVD has a beep tone to mark the four-second point that you can use as a cue to begin delayed repetition. Concentrate on accurate repetition of each number you hear. After you have finished repeating this exercise, turn off your recorder and answer the study questions. Remember, during this exercise you are not required to remember the content what you repeated.

Study Questions

1. Listen to the recording of your voice. Was repetition of a speech with numbers more difficult than immediate or delayed repetition? Why or why not?

____

____

____

2. Did you make any comments that the speaker did not make? If you did, how did those additions affect the message?

3. Was your spoken English intelligible? Did your words match the speaker's? Did your message match the speaker's? Were you able to maintain uniform control of the volume of your voice during the exercise?

4. Did errors in repeating any of the numbers affect the meaning? How?

5. Listen to the recording of yourself while reading the transcript. Circle the places on the transcript where you were not able to correctly repeat the numbers. If you lost your place during the repetition process, what caused that and how did you find your place again? Repeat the exercise and see if your ability to repeat the numbers correctly is improved when you are more familiar with the material.

Transcript for *How to Make a DNA Plasmid,* Pam Crisostomo

My name is Pam Crisostomo and this summer I've been working at a lab in—at UCSD [beep]. Um, basically my job has been to isolate plasma DNA for injections. Um, injections for mice, that is. Um, I'm a double-major at Stanford, or at least I hope to be. At this point I'm undeclared. And so I'm majoring in Bio and eventually I want to go to med school.

So volunteering at a laboratory seemed like a pretty good idea and I've actually learned a phenomenal amount. I came into the lab at ground zero, knowing nothing about molecu—molecular bio and now I just—I've learned a lot this summer.

Um, so, my job is to make DNA, basically and in order to make DNA I need to go through two major steps. And the first step is growing up the bugs or bacteria and second step is um, going through a process which breaks down the bugs, breaks down the bacteria, the cell walls and removes the proteins and stuff and—and then isolate the DNA from that. Um, so what I'm gonna describe is how to—how to start a culture of DNA—start a small culture of DNA and that's called inoculation.

So the first thing I need to do is I need to um, figure out what number the plasmid is, for example today my boss told me, um, to—that I'd have to make a culture of NCMV-B71 tomorrow. So in order to do that I need, uh, I need to grow the bugs up overnight. And so I go into her catalogue of DNA and the number for B - NCMV-B71 is number 32. And so I need to remember that number, because when I go into the freezer there's a lot of DNA, um, into—in little tubes and with certain numbers on them and so rather than wasting my time looking through, like, looking on the labels of all the tubes there's numbers on the top so I just remember the number 32.

And so the first thing that Delphine taught me was to, um, label everything. So I get a piece of colored tape and write the number 32. You need three things on—um, when you label: you need the name of what it is, the date and your initials. And so I put #32, NCMV-B71, um, the date is 8-27-96 and P.C. are my initials, and I stick the colored tape on a 3 mil (um, mil is milliliter) um, and actually I get a 10 mil culture tube and I aliquot 3 mils of LB into it.

And LB is luria broth and luria broth is the media for which, um, the media in which the bacteria grow—the bugs grow. And so I aliquot 3 mils of LB into the culture tube, um, and in order to aliquot that amount we need to be precise so we have a—a tool called the pipette aid and it's kind of a suction thing. In chemistry you used bulbs but this is a, more of a mechanic thing. And we stick the pipette into the—into the pipette aid and suction up 3 mils of LB and then we put 3 mils of this LB into the culture tube.

And after that, um, I need—this plasmid has to be ampicillin resistant, so we go into the freezer and in my box I have, um, a little tube of A-100 and A-100 stands for ampicillin, 100 mg per mililiter. And so since this is frozen I need to take the ampicillin out of the freezer and put it, on the heat block in order to thaw it, because you can't—you can't remove things out of—you can't pipette out of something that's frozen. So I put it on the heat block and once it's thawed I get a different thing called a pipette men. Which is—it's blue and you use it to pipette, um, small amounts up. And so I pipette up 3 microliters which is—we call them, um, written it's called lambda

(LMBDA) and that's a Greek letter. And, um, we—I pipette 3 LMBDA of, um, the thawed ampicillin and aliquot that, um, inject that into—into the 3 mils of LB. And so now any bacteria or any bugs I grow in this LB will be ampicillin resistant. And so then I make sure to put that back in the freezer because that needs to be frozen and it can't be left outside.

And then after that's ready I make sure the cap is on and the label is on, make sure everything's o.k. And then I need to go into the freezer room in order to get my bugs. So now that the media's ready and the culture tube is ready and everything's labeled, then I go into the freezer room and the bacteria is stored at -80 degrees celsius so I make sure before I—before I start and, um, always have my gloves on because, um, these things are biohazardous. So I take, um, I take my tray where I have my 10 mil culture tube and then I take um, my pipette (unintelligible), a box of pipette tips and also, um, and that's it. And then I go into the freezer room and I open the -80 degree freezer and I pull up, um, the box that—the deep box where the, um, where the, um, where the bacteria is stored. And so then I pull out the box and then I look for number 32. So then I take out my little tube which has #32 on it and I put—and then I put the rest of the box—I close the box and put it back in the freezer, 'cause you don't want all the other things to be thawing out at once. So you make sure to close that. And then, so I have my pipette with my box of pipette tips. And then so I scrape a little bit—I—using my pipette tip, I scrape a little bit of the NCMV-B71, um, with the end of my tip and put a little chunk of that into—into the 3 mils of LB plus amp. So then I put that in there and then I pipette up and pipette down in order to remove anything that might have gotten stuck in the pipette. And then, um, if—if the glycerol stock has been—is too frozen and you can't isolate a chunk then you remove—then you take out some of the LB. You pipette up and squirt some of that room temperature LB into the frozen glycerol stock in order to, um, soften it so you have kind of like a slushy mush. And then you can, um, remove some of the—the bacteria that's frozen there because it's softened and then you can remove a chunk from there. So then after you've done that you scrape a little bit and then put it into the—into the LB amp and then you cover—you twist the cover back on and put it back in the—80 degree freezer so only that has maybe chilled a little bit; gotten maybe a little bit warmer. So then you put it back, make sure nothing else has thawed. And then, so you have that into solution because it, um, defrosts pretty quickly so you have your bugs in solution and then you make sure to dispose of your pipette tip in the biohazardous waste because, um, it's biohazardous and you don't want anything um, else to be growing out of there. And then you take the 3 mil culture tube that's labeled and you put it into the shaker room. And the shaker room is where my bugs will grow overnight, but when I'm doing a small culture, um, first of all you need to turn down—you need to turn down the shaker so that it's not turning so fast. And then you turn it down and then you wait 'til it comes to a complete stop and after that you put the—put the 10 mil culture tube on the shaker, then you turn it up and you close the door; um, it's kept at 37 degrees and so you make sure that the shaker comes on again because a lot of people have different stuff growing on there. And after that, um, after it's done then you've already—you let it incubate for about 6 or 7 hours or, y'know, however long you're working there. And so, you need to inoculate a big culture, and right before you leave, um, you take the small culture (you have 3 mils) and then you—you take the small culture and separate that—

Five-Step Follow-up

Step 1 Observation

Review your answers to the study questions.

Step 2 Selection

Refer to your answers to Study Question 5 where you circled the places where the number repetition was inaccurate. For each circle, determine the effect of the error on the message. Was it serious or not serious?

____

____

____

____

Step 3 Analysis

Analyze your answer to step 2 more closely. Note how many numbers were omitted. Note if another number was substituted for the correct number. In cases where you substituted a number, was the substitution close to the original number in ordinal sequence?

____

____

____

____

Step 4 Assessment

What effect did errors in number repetition have on the meaning of the overall message? If the volume of your voice dropped off during number repetition, how did that affect the message? Was the rest of your repetition accurate, apart from the number repetition? Assess your work and determine if errors in repetition of the message followed errors in number repetition.

____

____

____

____

Step 5 Action

Develop a plan for action based on your analysis and assessment. For example, practice number repetition until you have found a way to repeat accurately. Incorporate the repetition strategies from immediate repetition to help you do this. If your performance included nonverbal movements, work to eliminate those in future practice. If your work included comments from you about your work, work to eliminate those comments in future practice. Practice this exercise again, and instead of immediate repetition use delayed repetition.

____

____

____

____

Progress Tracking Sheet

This sheet is designed to help you keep track of which exercises you have completed and how well you have done on these exercises. See page 12 for a full description of how to use the Progress Tracking Sheet.

Exercise Number	Date	First Performance	Study Questions	Follow-up Activity	Questions and Reminders	Date	Second Performance
Exercise 6.1 Quantitative							
Qualitative							
Exercise 6.2 Quantitative							
Qualitative							
Exercise 6.3 Quantitative							
Qualitative							
Quantitative Totals							

UNIT 7

Word-Level Pattern Inference

Introduction

A pattern is defined by Funk & Wagnall's dictionary as a model or original used as an archetype, or a model to be followed in making things. Inference means the act of deriving logical conclusions from information known to be true or reasoning from factual knowledge or evidence. Here, the term *word-level pattern inference* refers to the ability to complete a word pattern based on context provided. Another way to think of this concept is filling in the blank in a sentence with a word that makes sense in that context.

Pattern inference drills are those in which a word is deleted and the listener must fill in the missing word with a word that makes sense in that context. This task was originally called *cloze* and was used to evaluate levels of comprehension of words in sentences. (Oller, 1988) Typically cloze drills are written materials in which every fifth to tenth word is deleted. In order to fill in the missing word, the reader of the written passage must have a good enough knowledge of the language to know which word would logically fit in the blank without changing the meaning of the sentence. If the reader can do this, that reader knows the patterns of that language well enough to fill in the missing words. The value of pattern inference at the word level is that it indicates the presence of linguistic synthesis abilities. This synthesis is the ability that allows listeners to make sense of what they are hearing, even if they miss a word or part of word. In general, word-level pattern inference ability is present for those who have good levels of language proficiency. Since interpreters need high levels of language proficiency, it is important to develop this specific skill.

The Role of Word-Level Pattern Inference in the Interpretation Process

In interpreter education programs, this kind of "missing word" drill often appears as a spoken language drill and is used to develop linguistic abilities that are needed in the interpretation process. Pattern inference skills can be demonstrated at two different levels. One is the idea level. At this level you would ask yourself what ideas or concepts would fit in the blank. The other level is grammatical. At this level you ask yourself which word or kind of word would make sense in the blank. Sometimes the blank can be filled in with only one word and other times a variety of words will make sense. The presence of pattern inference skills at the word level means that the listener has enough linguistic skill to make logical inferences as to which word could reasonably be used to complete the idea. It is important to stress that this is not based on guesswork, but rather on comprehension of the English language. Pattern inference skills are valuable in training and in the real world of interpreting. Good pattern inference skills can help distinguish homonyms such as "fair" and "fare." By relying on context and having strong language skills, you will know which word is the one the speaker intended. Sometimes people are not aware that they have the ability to use pattern inference skills. By practicing the written and spoken drills in this text, you can become more aware of your own pattern inference skills.

Interpreters often must deal with auditory distractions that interfere with the listening process. These distractions can include noises that override or block out the message to which they are listening. For example, if a plane flies overhead or a door slams, the interpreter may miss part of what the speaker said. When this happens, it is often possible to continue without stopping the speaker. It is likely that the interpreter will be able to "fill in the blank" if good pattern inference skills are in place. The ability to fill in the blank is less likely to be present during speeches that contain technical information or vocabulary that is unknown to the interpreter because technical speeches tend to have patterns that are not widely known to those outside of that technical specialty. The more familiar the interpreter is with the topic, the greater the chance that the interpreter will be able to use word-level pattern inference skills.

In this unit, two kinds of word-level pattern inference exercises are provided. First, eight written exercises are presented. Then three word-level pattern inference exercises based on spoken material are presented. Complete the written exercises first. Fill in the blank with a word that makes sense in the context of that story. Think of as many words as you can that make sense in this context and write them down, too. Then go on to the spoken exercises.

Word-Level Pattern Inference Exercises with Written Material

Directions

Fill in the blank with a word that makes sense in the context of the story. In most cases you will supply a single word. Do not worry about supplying the "right" word. It must be a word that makes sense and could logically be used in that selection. Read the entire selection before making your decision.

EXERCISE 1.

A Trip to the Vet

Context: This is a passage about when Suzanne's dog got sick.

1. I have a friend named Suzanne. Her dog's name is Brownie.
2. The dog had ______________________ so she took him to the vet.
3. The vet ______________________ Brownie and found fleas.
4. The vet gave Brownie a ______________________ and flea powder.
5. Now, Brownie ______________________ flea powder but feels better.

EXERCISE 2.

Breakfast at a Restaurant

Context: This is a passage about breakfast at a small cafe.

1. My favorite ______________________ is the Teacup Cafe.
2. It is on the ______________________ of Glacier and Zircon in the town of Grand Forks.
3. I like this restaurant most because the ______________________ is shaped like a giant teacup.

4. It is a breakfast ______________________ and is open from 5:00 a.m. until 11:00 a.m.

5. When I go there I always order sausage patties, ______________, and wheat toast.

6. I drink ______________________ tea with my food.

7. My favorite waitress is Marge. She always gives me the news of the ______________________, so I always give her a big tip.

EXERCISE 3.

Peter's New Boat

Context: This is a passage about Peter, who is looking for a boat.

1. Peter has become ______________________ as a used car dealer.

2. He has a two story condo in Southern California and ______________ a second hand Jeep Grand Cherokee.

3. Now he is interested in a new ______________________: sailing.

4. Last semester he took two ______________________ at a local college.

5. One was "Elements of Navigation" and the ______________ was "Fundamentals of Marine Safety."

6. Now he is shopping for a ______________________ yacht and hoping for a good deal.

7. Maybe he will find a ______________________.

EXERCISE 4.

A Visit to a Palm Reader

Context: Casey was on vacation in Vermont and went to have her fortune told.

1. My ______________________________ Casey is interested in New Age things.

2. Last week, she was in Vermont on ______________________________. She went to see a gypsy palm reader and fortuneteller for advice on a new career.

3. The fortuneteller's ______________________________ was Madame Cobra.

4. When Casey went into Madame Cobra's room, she smelled sandalwood ______________________________.

5. Casey saw an old woman wearing a velvet ______________________________ and a turban.

6. The woman looked in her crystal ______________________________ and helped Casey make a decision.

EXERCISE 5.

My New Back Yard

Context: This passage is about fixing up my new back yard.

1. I just bought a new ______________________________ in Columbia, Maryland.

2. It is a Victorian style house with a large ______________________________ and gingerbread trim.

3. It was built on a vacant lot. When I moved in the yard was wild and full of ______________________________. There was a lot of poison sumac.

4. I am allergic to the weeds so I ______________________ a landscape architect to plan a new weed-free yard.

5. The new yard is ______________________.

EXERCISE 6.

Visit to New Zealand

Context: Duane went to New Zealand last year.

1. Last year Duane had a one-month vacation, so he took a ____________ to New Zealand.

2. He took his vacation in December because New Zealand is in the ______________________ and has opposite seasons. So he was there for their summer.

3. New Zealand has two main islands. One is the south island and the other is the north island. Each is ______________________ by many volcanoes.

4. New Zealand was inhabited first by Polynesians called Maoris. Now it has many ______________________ as well.

5. It is very mountainous because of the New Zealand Alps. He enjoyed ______________________ there.

6. While there he saw one of the largest glaciers in the ______________.

7. Just over the mountains is a large rainforest where it ______________ more than twelve feet per year.

8. While in the rainforest he was ______________________. He saw a large colony of rare Yellow-eyed Penguins.

9. Penguins are one of the fifteen kinds of ______________________ birds in New Zealand.

EXERCISE 7.

Vacation on the Coast of Mexico

Context: My vacation last year was on the Caribbean coast of Mexico.

1. I have always wanted to see the Caribbean, but I am a workaholic and never took a ______________________.
2. Finally, last ______________________ on our honeymoon, I saw the Caribbean coast of Mexico.
3. We went to the island of Cozumel, which is just south of Cancun but is more ______________________.
4. We stayed in a small ______________________ that looked like a hacienda.
5. While I was there I learned to ______________________ in the beautiful blue water.
6. The water is very salty and very warm so it is very ____________.
7. I spent most of every day lying in the water watching the ______________________. I especially liked the parrotfish and the barracudas.
8. One night my husband caught several abalone. We cooked and ate them. It was a ______________________ I'll never forget.

EXERCISE 8.

Frank's Trip to the Doctor

Context: Frank went to the doctor for his yearly checkup.

1. This year Frank turned forty and went to the ______________________ for his annual checkup.
2. His doctor is a(n) ______________________ who specializes in family medicine.
3. The night before his ______________________, Frank had to fast.

4. At the clinic he had an EKG and a ______________________ test for everything, including TB.

5. They found that he has a heart ______________________ and his cholesterol and blood pressure are too high.

6. Now he is on a low-fat, low-sodium ______________________ and he has joined an aerobics class.

For additional practice with written pattern inference exercises, go to the World Wide Web and look up "cloze."

Word-Level Pattern Inference Exercises with Spoken Material

EXERCISE 7.1

A Childhood Memory

CHRIS LEWNES

Directions

It will take approximately two minutes to do this exercise. After completing the exercise answer the questions and do the follow-up exercises. Turn on the DVD player and find this selection. Take time to look at the title and speaker's face before proceeding with the exercise. Think about what possible ideas may be presented by this speaker in relation to this topic.

You can complete this exercise in one of two ways. Preferably, you will record your spoken answers by using a video camera or a tape recorder. To do this, find this selection on the DVD and prepare your recording device with enough blank tape to record your answers. Turn on your recording device first and then turn on the DVD player.

As soon as you hear the beep tone you should say a word or two that makes sense and is loud enough for your recorder to pick up both the speaker's voice and your voice. During this exercise it is important to cut off the "inner critic," or the tendency to criticize yourself either silently or out loud. You will distract yourself and lose precious time if you criticize yourself instead of concentrating on the message. When you hear the beep, say a word that would make sense in that context.

If you realize a few seconds later that another word would make better sense there, then say that word and keep listening to the message and for the next beep. This process of inserting a more appropriate word is the process of self-correction. Your recording will have both of your responses.

The second and less preferred way to respond to the exercise is as follows: if you are not working in an environment that will allow you to say your answers out loud, then you can listen to the speaker and write your answers, as soon as you hear the beep, in the space provided in the transcript.

Study Questions

1. Read the transcript while listening to your recording. Write your answers from the recording in the space provided in the transcript.

2. Compare your answers with the words that were deleted from the transcript. The words deleted from the transcript are listed at the end of the transcript. For each missing word that you filled in, state how you decided what kind of information would logically fit in the blank.

____

____

____

____

____

____

____

____

____

____

____

____

3. Circle any answers that do not make sense. Put a double underline under your answers that do make sense. Replace any circled words with words that do make sense in this context.

4. Check a thesaurus for other words that could be used for each word deleted from the transcript. Write down the synonyms for words that could be used in this context without changing the meaning.

   ____

   ____

5. The term *register* refers to the level of formality of the language. Are your answers in the same register as those of the original or are they more or less formal? If any of your answers are in a different register, does the register variation change the meaning?

   ____

   ____

   ____

Transcript for *A Childhood Memory,* Chris Lewnes

Hello. My name is Chris Lewnes. I'd like to talk about a fond memory that I had from childhood. As I recall, I was ten years old, on my way home from *1.*______________________________ and on a street corner was my favorite aunt. It was a surprise to me because she didn't 2.______________________________ in that town and I hadn't seen her that often. When she 3.________________________ me she asked me if I wanted to go with her to Washington, D.C. I was real surprised. At that *4.*______________________________ I had never been more than a hundred miles from my home. And Washington was a good 250 miles away. We left that 5.______________________________ on a train. I'd never been on a train before that *6.*____________________. Got to Washington—as I recall it must have been about 11:00 in the *7.*____________________ Washington was a beautiful sight—all lit up at night.

The next day I got to see the Capitol, the White House, the *8.*____________________; however my aunt was more interested in seeing the National Museum of Art, so she *9.*____________________ me over and I had to sit there for hours while she enjoyed the—while she enjoyed the *10.*____________________. Of course, I was too young at the time to appreciate it. But it was a *11.*____________________ experience for me, and one that I've *12.*____________________ all these years fondly.

Answer Key

1. *school*
2. *live*
3. *greeted*
4. *time*
5. *evening*
6. *distance*
7. *evening*
8. *Washington Monument*
9. *dragged*
10. *artwork*
11. *memorable*
12. *remembered*

Five-Step Follow-up

Step 1 Observation

Review your answers to the study questions.

Step 2 **Selection**

Refer to your answer to Study Question 3. The circled words are those that do not make sense in this context.

Step 3 **Analysis**

For each circled word, state why it does not make sense. State why you chose the word you did. Refer to a thesaurus to make sure that the words you have selected to replace the circled words make sense in this context. List as many words as possible that could be used in this context.

____

____

____

____

Step 4 **Assessment**

What effect did errors have on the meaning of the overall message? Evaluate the effect of the errors in terms of "serious" or "not serious." A serious error means that the original meaning of the message was lost. A nonserious error may change the meaning slightly, but the meaning would still be understood in generally the same way as the original message.

____

____

____

____

Step 5 **Action**

Develop a plan for action based on your analysis and assessment. Once you have determined the effect of word choices on the meaning of the message, you can work to develop rapid and accurate word-level pattern inference skills. One way to develop this skill with written material is to look up "cloze" exercises on the World Wide Web. You can practice with spoken material by working with a friend who can read from a magazine or book and omit every fifth to tenth word. The reader should mark the words that are omitted. Use a tape recorder to record your work and check it for accuracy by comparing your recording with the printed material that was used. You can use the study questions and follow-up to check your work.

EXERCISE 7.2

A Frightening Experience

RICHARD SOMERVILLE

Directions

It will take approximately three minutes to do this exercise. After completing the exercise answer the study questions and do the follow-up exercises. Turn on the DVD player and find this selection. Take time to look at the title and the speaker's face before proceeding with the exercise. Think about what possible ideas may be presented by this speaker on this topic.

You can complete this exercise in one of two ways. Preferably, you will record your spoken answers by using a video camera or a tape recorder. To do this, find the selection on the DVD and prepare your recording device with enough blank tape to record your answers. Turn on your recording device first and then turn on the DVD player.

As soon as you hear the beep tone you should say a word or two that makes sense and is loud enough for your recorder to pick up both the speaker's voice and your voice. During this exercise it is important to cut off the "inner critic," or the tendency to criticize yourself either silently or out loud. You will distract yourself and lose precious time if you criticize yourself instead of concentrating on the message. When you hear the beep, say a word that would make sense in that spot.

If you realize a few seconds later that another word would make better sense there, then say that word and keep listening to the message and for the next beep. This process of inserting a more appropriate word is the process of self-correction. Your recording will have both of your responses.

The second and less preferred way to respond to the exercise is as follows: if you are not working in an environment that will allow you to say your answers out loud, then you can listen to the speaker and write your answers, as soon as you hear the beep, in the space provided in the transcript.

Study Questions

1. Read the transcript while listening to your recording. Write your answers from your recording in the space provided in the transcript.

2. Compare your answers with the words that were deleted from the transcript. The words deleted from the transcript are listed at the end of the transcript. Select 10 of the answers you wrote and state how you decided what kind of information would logically fit in the blank.

____

____

____

____

____

____

____

____

____

____

3. Circle any answers that do not make sense. Put a double underline under your answers that do make sense. Replace any circled words with words that do make sense in this context.

4. Check a thesaurus for other words that could be used for each word that is missing from the transcript. Write down the synonyms for words that could be used in this context without changing the meaning.

____

____

____

____

5. The term *register* refers to the level of formality of the language. Are your answers in the same register as those of the original or are they more or less formal? If any of your answers are in a different register, does the register variation change the meaning?

____

____

____

____

Transcript for *A Frightening Experience*, Richard Somerville

My name is Richard Somerville. I want to tell you about a frightening experience that I had some years ago when my youngest son was just a toddler. We were vacationing in the Adriatic Ocean off, uh, Yugoslavia and he had a boating accident while my wife and I were away. He fell on the boat and cut his head badly, and was *1.*____________________ profusely. It was a tiny village in a very 2.____________________ place, and the nurse at the first aid station 3.____________________ he had broken his skull. She didn't speak 4.____________________ and we didn't speak Serbo-Croatian so we were 5.____________________ with her in German, but she was very clear that our son had 6.____________________ his skull and he had to be taken by ambulance to a 7.____________________. That was one of the most 8.____________________ rides I've ever had. The Yugoslav ambulance driver was a wild and 9.____________________

man who drove madly on the wrong side of the road, on the side, uh, where cars shouldn't be, and uh, passed *10.*__________________, sirens flashing—screaming sirens, lights flashing... and it was, uh, a ride that seemed to last *11.*__________________. Uh, I was following behind him in a car they wouldn't let me ride in the *12.*__________________ so I was also driving at terrifying speeds and, uh, I was *13.*__________________ first of all that my son was going to *14.*__________________ from having a fractured skull and second that my *15.*__________________ and I were going to get killed in a terrible *16.*__________________. It just seemed impossible to me that we'd make it. We were going over tiny mountain roads, two-lane *17.*__________________, going around blind curves on the wrong side of the road. And we ended up in the hospital of a nearby *18.*__________________. And after a long time the doctor, who also spoke *19.*__________________, came out and told us that he didn't have a *20.*__________________ skull after all, he just had a bad cut, he'd been sewed up, the *21.*__________________ had stopped, there wasn't anything wrong with him, and, uh, he was going to recover and be *22.*__________________. It took me a long time to get my *23.*__________________ back that night, and I think if I have to draw a *24.*__________________ from that terrible experience it's uh, not to believe that things are always going to be as bad as they *25.*__________________ sometimes they turn out to be a lot better.

Answer Key

1. *bleeding*
2. *primitive*
3. *thought*
4. *English*
5. *communicating*
6. *broken*
7. *hospital*
8. *terrifying*
9. *crazy*
10. *everybody*
11. *forever*
12. *ambulance*
13. *afraid*
14. *die*
15. *wife*
16. *accident*
17. *highways*
18. *city*
19. *German*
20. *fractured*
21. *bleeding*
22. *fine*
23. *equilibrium*
24. *moral*
25. *seem*

Five-Step Follow-up

Step 1 Observation

Review your answers to the study questions.

Step 2 Selection

Refer to your answer to Study Question 3. The circled words are those that do not make sense in this context.

Step 3 Analysis

For each circled word, state why it does not make sense. State why you chose the word you did. Refer to a thesaurus to make sure that the words you have selected to replace the circled words make sense in this context. List as many words as possible that could be used in this context.

____

____

____

____

Step 4 Assessment

What effect did errors have on the meaning of the overall message? Evaluate the effect of the errors in terms of "serious" or "nonserious." A serious error means that the original meaning of the message was lost. A not serious error may change the meaning slightly, but the meaning would still be understood in generally the same way as the meaning of the original message.

____

____

____

____

Step 5 Action

Develop a plan for action based on your analysis and assessment. Once you have determined the effect of word choices on the meaning of the message, you can work to develop rapid and accurate word-level pattern inference skills. One way to develop this skill with written material is to look up "cloze" exercises on the World Wide Web. You can practice with spoken material by working with a friend who can read from a magazine or book and omit every fifth to tenth word. The reader should mark the words that are omitted. Use a tape recorder to record your work and check it for accuracy by comparing your recording with the printed material that was used. You can use the study questions and follow-up to check your work.

____

____

____

____

EXERCISE 7.3

How to Make a Greek Appetizer

MAUREEN LEWNES

Directions

It will take approximately five minutes to do the exercise. After completing the exercise answer the study questions, then do the follow-up exercises. Turn on the DVD player and find this selection. Take time to look at the title and the speaker's face before proceeding with the exercise. Think about what possible ideas may be presented by this speaker. This topic may be unfamiliar to you. Do your best to provide answers that make sense as soon as you hear the beeps. Correct yourself as soon as you realize you need to.

You can complete this exercise in one of two ways. Preferably, you will record your spoken answers by using a video camera or a tape recorder. To do this, find this selection on the DVD and prepare your recording device with enough blank tape to record your answers. Turn on your recording device first and then turn on the DVD player.

As soon as you hear the beep tone, you should say a word or two that makes sense and is loud enough for your recorder to pick up both the speaker's voice and your voice. During this exercise it is important to cut off the "inner critic," or the tendency to criticize yourself either silently or out loud. You will distract yourself and lose precious time if you criticize yourself instead of concentrating on the message. When you hear the beep, say a word that would make sense in that spot. If you realize a few seconds later that another word would make better sense there, then say that word and keep listening to the message and for the next beep. This process of inserting a more appropriate word is the process of self-correction. Your recording will have both of your responses.

The second and less preferred way to respond to the exercise is as follows: if you are not working in an environment that will allow you to say your answers out loud, then you can listen to the speaker and write your answers, as soon as you hear the beep, in the space provided below.

Study Questions

1. Read the transcript while listening to your recording. Write your answers from the recording in the space provided in the transcript.

2. Compare your answers with the words that were deleted from the transcript. The words deleted from the transcript are listed at the end of the transcript. For 10 of the missing words that you filled in, state how you decided what kind of information would logically fit in the blank.

3. Circle any answers that do not make sense. Put a double underline under your answers that do make sense. Replace any circled words with words that do make sense in this context.

4. Check a thesaurus for other words that could be used for each word in the word list at the end of the transcript. Write down the synonyms for words that could be used in this context without changing the meaning.

5. The term *register* refers to the level of formality of the language. Are your answers in the same register as those of the original, or are they more or less formal? If any of your answers are in a different register, does the register variation change the meaning?

____

____

____

____

Transcript for *How to Make a Greek Appetizer,* Maureen Lewnes

Hello. My name is Maureen Lewnes. Uh, today I'm going to share with you how to make, uh, an appetizer that is called tiropites. This appetizer comes from the Greek culture. It is made of cheese and it, um, is surrounded by a dough called phyllo dough. You can find phyllo dough in the *1.*______________ section of your supermarket. Take it home and store it overnight to thaw in your regular 2.______________. When you remove the phyllo dough from the refrigerator you will need to 3.______________ to keep it covered or sealed, 'cause it is like tissue paper and it dries out very easily. Uh, you'll need to cover it with a damp towel, uh, to keep the dough 4.______________ and easy to work with. You will need to, uh, initially, uh, cut the phyllo dough into strips about 3 inches wide and, um, keep them under the 5.______________ until you're ready to, uh, fill it with your filling. The filling that we will make is made of, uh, three kinds of cheese. The first cheese is a feta cheese. You'll need one 6.______________ of feta cheese, which is a Greek goat cheese. Um, it's also found in other 7.______________ such as Denmark, and there is now a domestic production of feta in the United States. The feta cheese is very strong, so we want to, um, *8.*____________________ that flavor, and we will add four beaten *9.*____________________ to the crumbled feta cheese. The feta cheese can be crumbled with a fork and then, um, after you've added the one—cup of feta cheese and the four beaten eggs you will need to *10.*____________________ a half a cup of small curd cottage cheese. With the cottage cheese you might want to add approx— approximately an eighth of a teaspoon of pepper. You will also need for the third cheese an eighth of a cup of um, kefalotyri cheese, which is another Greek cheese. If this is unavailable to you, you can *11.*____________________ blue cheese for the kefolotiri. First thing you want to do is lay a strip on your counter top of the phyllo dough. I usually lay down a piece of wax paper, as the phyllo is less likely to *12.*____________________ to the counter top. Um, brush the phyllo with a mixture of a half a cup of melted butter and a half a cup of oil that has been blended. I use a pastry *13.*____________________ and lightly brush the phyllo. After you've laid the one strip down and buttered it you can take a second *14.*____________________ and lay over the top of the first strip. Um, you could go on and add three or four layers, whatever your personal taste is—I usually use approximately two layers. Then at the very *15.*____________________ or bottom of the strip, take a teaspoon of the cheese *16.*____________________ that you have in the small bowl and place this on the end of the strip. Take and roll up, um, about two inches of the phyllo *17.*____________________ over the, uh, cheese mixture and then continue to fold in a flag *18.*____________________ until you have a triangle. The very end of the dough needs to be *19.*____________________ with the butter mixture. You need to put this on a buttered, uh, cookie sheet and then brush the top lightly with the butter. It sounds like a lot of butter, but you need to do it in a light-handed fashion. Um, after you've filled the cookie *20.*____________ with, uh, several triangles you'll need to bake this in a 375-degree preheated oven. Um, as ovens vary in *21.*____________ it's a good idea to keep an eye on it after 10 minutes. Um, it will brown fairly quickly and sometimes the cheese will *22.*____________ out of the corners. But you will be the rave of the *23.*____________ with these new, uh, tiropites appetizers. I hope you *24.*____________ tiropites.

Answer Key

The words that Maureen Lewnes actually used are in the left column and possible synonyms, or words that would make sense in this context, are to the right.

1. *freezer*
2. *refrigerator*
3. *remember*
4. *moist*
5. *towel*
6. *cup*
7. *countries*
8. *dilute*
9. *eggs*
10. *add*
11. *substitute*
12. *stick*
13. *brush*
14. *strip*
15. *end*
16. *mixture*
17. *dough*
18. *fashion*

19. *sealed*
20. *tray*
21. *temperature*
22. *ooze*
23. *neighborhood*
24. *enjoy*

Five-Step Follow-up

Step 1 Observation

Review your answers to the study questions.

Step 2 Selection

Refer to your answer to Study Question 3. The circled words are those that do not make sense in this context.

Step 3 Analysis

For each circled word, state why it does not make sense. State why you chose the word you did. Refer to a thesaurus to make sure that the words you have selected to replace the circled words make sense in this context. List as many words as possible that could be used in this context.

____

____

____

____

Step 4 Assessment

What effect did errors have on the meaning of the overall message? Evaluate the effect of the errors in terms of "serious" or "not serious." A serious error means that the original meaning of the message was lost. A nonserious error may change the meaning slightly, but the meaning would still be understood in generally the same way as the original message.

____

____

Step 5 Action

Develop a plan for action based on your analysis and assessment. Once you have determined the effect of word choices on the meaning of the message, you can work to develop rapid and accurate word-level pattern inference skills. One way to develop this skill with written material is to look up "cloze" exercises on the World Wide Web. You can practice with spoken material by working with a friend who can read from a magazine or book and omit every fifth to tenth word. The reader should mark the words that are omitted. Use a tape recorder to record your work and check it for accuracy by comparing your recording with the printed material that was used. You can use the study questions and follow-up to check your work.

Progress Tracking Sheet

This sheet is designed to help you keep track of which exercises you have completed and how well you have done on these exercises. See page 12 for a full description of how to use the Progress Tracking Sheet.

Exercise Number	Date	First Performance	Study Questions	Follow-up Activity	Questions and Reminders	Date	Second Performance
Exercise 7.1 Quantitative							
Qualitative							
Exercise 7.2 Quantitative							
Qualitative							
Exercise 7.3 Quantitative							
Qualitative							
Quantitative Totals							

UNIT 8

Phrase-Level Pattern Inference

Introduction

Phrase-level pattern inference in spoken English is the ability to complete a sentence, idea, or text with a logical ending. These pattern completion skills are based on having strong linguistic skills and on being able to use context to find possible and logical solutions. Pattern inference skills at the phrase level form another subset of skills that are necessary for both interpreters in training and working interpreters. Oller (1988) describes the ability to complete linguistic patterns as "active hypothesis testing." Thus, completion involves more than just guessing what would come next in the speech. The interpreter needs to check a hypothesis against what has already been heard and see if this hypothesis is a possible and logical direction for the speech to follow. The completion process also has a retroactive component. Once the active hypothesis has been made, the listener checks the actual speech to see if the hypothesis is supported.

There are two broad categories within this skill. One is short-term pattern inference, which allows for logical completion of sentences or other short idea units, such as phrases. The other is long-term pattern inference, which allows for logical completion of longer texts such as paragraphs or speeches. As mentioned in Unit 7, pattern inference skills occur at the grammatical level and at the idea level.

An example of how pattern inference skills work at the grammatical level can be seen in collocations. Collocations are phrases or groups of words that occur in a predictable pattern. Larson (1984) says "Some words occur together often, other words may occur together occasionally, and some combination of words are not likely to occur. Knowing which words go together is an important part of understanding the meaning of a text" (p. 141). Larson says that *collocate* means to put side by side. Larson provides the following definition of collocations. "Collocations are words joined together in phrases or sentences to form semantically unified expressions. The combination which forms a semantically correct meaning in one language may not do so in another" (p. 144). Different languages have different word combinations that are acceptable.

According to Larson there are several types of collocations. One type is fixed collocations. Fixed collocations always occur in the same order and are often idiomatic expressions. For example, the phrase "has the cat got your ____________________?" is almost always finished with "tongue." You always expect to hear it the same way, and at the same time the meaning of the question is not revealed by the actual words. You need to know that it means, "Why are you so quiet?" or "Why don't you answer?" Other collocations are not fixed, but rely on how the grammar of the language works. Larson uses the following examples to illustrate this point. She says that in English you would say "I had a dream," but in Russian you would say "I saw in a dream." Another example is the grammatical construction "not only..., but also...." If the listener hears "not only," one logical hypothesis is that the speaker will soon say "but also." For more information on collocations, refer to *Meaning Based Translation Skills,* by Mildred Larson.

So in order to work on phrase-level pattern inference, you will need two things. First is a good command of spoken English and its grammatically acceptable constructions. Second, you will need the ability to logically complete an idea based on the context and the information you have heard up to the point where the phrase ends.

The Role of Phrase-Level Pattern Inference Skills in the Interpretation Process

Well-developed pattern inference skills will allow the interpreter to hypothesize how a sentence, paragraph, or longer text might logically be completed. This is important because interpreters are usually planning ahead and exploring possible directions that the speech may follow while interpreting. Pattern inference skills are positively related to world knowledge. The greater your world knowledge and the larger your stores of schemas or information patterns for how things work, the greater the likelihood that your set of possibilities will contain an appropriate choice. This kind of important information is generally based on prior knowledge. In other words, the more you know about how things work, the more likely you will be able to hypothesize logical endings for the speeches you will hear. The more practice and awareness you have of the importance of phrase-level pattern inference, the less effort you will need to devote to this aspect of the interpretation process.

In general, it is more likely that pattern inference skills will be accurate if the interpreter has an already established schema or general frame of reference for an idea. For example, if a person listening to their mechanic already knows how an automobile engine works, then that person will more likely be able to create predictions that are in line with the speaker's intent. This is not to say that interpreters should create their own endings to sentences or stories, but rather that they should use active hypothesis testing to prepare their minds for the probable directions of the speech. Accurate and reliable pattern inference skills will allow greater capacity management during the interpretation process. As noted by Gile (1995), the greater the capacity for the components of the interpretation processes, including pattern inference skills, the more likely that the interpreter will have adequate cognitive capacity to manage the entire simultaneous interpretation processes.

If good pattern inference and hypothesis testing skills are in place, they may indicate that the interpreter has access to basic reasoning ability and logic. Pattern inference skills are directly related to simultaneous interpretation, even though in the training sequence basic pattern inference and simultaneous interpretation are quite far apart. Reliable pattern inference skills help the interpreter follow the speaker's line of reasoning. The interpreter benefits from being able to order the ideas and rank them in importance as well as by selecting the main point and supporting points. Alternatively, because not all speakers make sense, it is important to be able to note when there is no clear line of reasoning being used by the speaker.

Ability to Tolerate Ambiguity

As an interpreter develops good pattern inference skills, insight into how ideas fit together will help interpreters develop hypotheses about what the speaker will say. As the pattern inference skills develop, it is likely that the interpreter will become more sensitive to ambiguity. Ambiguity means that a word or phrase could have more than one meaning. Ideally, the context will allow the interpreter and other listeners to know which meaning is intended. But if not, then the interpreter's heightened sensitivity to possible meanings will allow them to know that there is more than one possible meaning. If context does not make it clear which meaning is intended and the interpreter is aware of this, the interpreter needs to stop the speaker to ask for clarification. Some ambiguity must be tolerated as the speaker reveals his or her point. Sometimes the speaker may not show or tell the interpreter how the ideas being presented are related, and this can add to the interpreter's cognitive load. Occasionally, stopping the speaker for clarification will not reduce the ambiguity for the interpreter or other listeners because there are times when the speaker does not really know what point he or she wants to make.

More experienced interpreters generally will be able to tolerate more ambiguity than those who are just learning. Moser (1997) suggests that one of the most notable differences between novice and expert interpreters is that the novices tend to be distracted by superficial problems along the way and use a more "microview" approach wherein they can get "lost" in the details. Expert interpreters, on the other hand, tend to use a more global approach, or a "macroview," which allows them to avoid getting lost in the details and therefore to follow the overall message better. Pattern inference skills help students of interpretation reach that macroview.

Phrase-Level Pattern Inference Exercises with Written Material

Directions

Read the context sentence for each story. Allow yourself a few moments to create a set of possible and logical hypotheses regarding the topic and context. Then read each sentence and fill in the blank with as many logical endings as you can.

EXERCISE 1.

Birdwatching

Context: William's hobby is birdwatching.

1. William's house is near a state forest preserve. His land borders on an old growth forest of ______________________________.
2. His yard is full of shrubs and bushes with berries and seeds for the birds to ______________________________.
3. He also has several bird feeders. One is filled with thistles and attracts ______________________________.
4. Another has sunflower seeds. Chickadees love ____________________.
5. The third feeder has safflower seeds for the ________________________ ______________________________.
6. William also has a wire holder for suet, a kind of fat that woodpeckers ______________________________.

7. So far, he has sighted fifty-four different species of wild birds and one parakeet that escaped from the ______________________.

EXERCISE 2.

Lois' Three Cats

Context: My neighbor Lois has three cats. This passage describes their antics.

1. My neighbor Lois is a cat lover. Her house is filled with ceramic cats, she has cat flags on her porch and she also has three ______________________.

2. The biggest cat is white and fluffy. Its name is Snow ______________________.

3. The cat acts like a spoiled princess and Lois waits on her like a ______________________.

4. The other two cats are calico cats. One has a very sweet disposition and the other ______________________.

5. One is named Grumpy and the other is named Sweetheart. Their personalities match their ______________________.

6. In the morning Grumpy bites Lois on the ankles until she ______________________.

7. Lois is considering getting another cat from the ______________________.

EXERCISE 3.

Treasure Hunt

Context: Treasures for your home can be found by hunting in various places.

1. My friend Sharon loves to hunt for bargains and find treasures in antique shops and ______________________.
2. She loves cobalt blue glass and other kinds of glass. Fortunately, she knows the value of many kinds of glass and knows how much to ______________________.
3. She went to an antique shop in Annapolis, Maryland. She found a cobalt glass owl and a beautiful lead crystal paperweight, faceted like a ______________________.
4. The same day she went to a garage sale near Baltimore. She found a special paperweight that was within her ______________________.
5. Now her garage is so full of treasures she will need to have a ______________________.

EXERCISE 4.

My Son's Pets

Context: My son has some exotic pets.

1. My son Mark is twelve years old. He keeps busy with various interests and ______________________.
2. He is interested in reptiles and other exotic ______________________ ______________________.
3. His first pet was a hamster. Later he got a Guinea ______________________ ______________________.
4. He is good about taking care of them. He gets old produce at the ______________________.
5. Recently he has become interested in ______________________ ______________________.

6. He just got a painted tortoise and it ______________________________.

7. He told me he wants to buy ______________________________.

8. But I said "no." I have a phobia about ______________________________ ______________________________.

EXERCISE 5.

Vacation in Atlantic City

Context: Our friends got a free vacation in Atlantic City.

1. Paula and Zach live in Youngstown, Pennsylvania, which is famous for steel mills. They both work ______________________________.

2. Paula works in public relations and Zach ______________________________ ______________________________.

3. This year they worked many extra hours and were given ______________ ______________________________.

4. They will go to the Jersey shore for ______________________________ ______________________________.

5. They will use a condo that belongs to ______________________________ ______________________________.

6. They plan to loaf on the beach during the day and enjoy the __________ ______________________________.

7. Zach likes to play roulette but Paula ______________________________.

8. They have tickets to see ______________________________.

9. On the way home they will stop at Six Flags amusement park and ______________________________.

EXERCISE 6.

Road Trip!

Context: Last weekend Renee went on an unplanned trip to New England.

1. On Sunday, Renee and her two friends Keith and Chris decided at the last minute to ______________________________.
2. They bought tickets and ______________________________.
3. They had dinner at an Italian restaurant called Hot Tomatoes. Renee doesn't like Italian food so she ______________________________.
4. Keith loves Italian food so he ______________________________.
5. Later they drove to Boston which they ______________________________ ______________________________.
6. Finally they drove to Cape Cod and saw ______________________________ and ______________________________.

EXERCISE 7.

A Trip to the Mechanic

Context: This is about Richard taking his car to the shop.

1. Last Tuesday, Richard was driving to work in Austin, Texas. A man waved at him and wrote a note to him saying that ______________________________ ______________________________.
2. Richard drove straight to the Texas Tire and Auto which is ______________________________.
3. Reuben, the mechanic, shook his head and said, "It sounds like your air conditioner. I hope it is only a ______________________________ but it ______________________________.
4. Richard went on to work on the bus and later he ______________________________ ______________________________.
5. Reuben told him it was the compressor and would ______________________________ ______________________________.

6. Richard decided he could be hot while in his car and ________________ ________________________________.

7. His car is old and ________________________________.

8. Now he is shopping for a ________________________________ which he will buy with ________________________________.

EXERCISE 8.

A Visit to the Emergency Room

Context: My friend was hurt at work and had to go to the hospital.

1. Last year my co-worker Bruce fell from a low scaffold and ____________ ________________________________.

2. When he landed he got a ________________________________ from a nail in a board.

3. The nail went through ________________________________ and stuck in his foot.

4. We called 911 and an ambulance and ________________________________ came in five minutes.

5. The EMT put Bruce on a gurney and ________________________________ and ________________________________.

6. In the emergency room the doctor ________________________________ and then the doctor ________________________________.

7. He gave Bruce a tetanus shot in the ________________________________ and some strong ________________________________.

8. Now they are making us wear ________________________________ at work.

EXERCISE 9.

Swimming

Context: Scott likes to swim for exercise.

1. Scott swims every day as ______________________.
2. He swims in the ______________________.
3. Today he had trouble getting enough swimming time. When he arrived, ______________________ so he had to wait.
4. Later, a water aerobics class began and that left ______________________ ______________________.
5. He shared a lane with a slow swimmer who ______________________ ______________________.
6. Finally, he got a lane alone and swam ______________________.

Phrase-Level Pattern Inference Exercises with Spoken Material

EXERCISE 8.1

My Favorite Teacher

MAUREEN LEWNES

Directions

In this two minute exercise, the speaker is interrupted with a beep tone. When you hear the beep, complete the phrase. Enough time is provided on the DVD for you to provide your answer if you answer promptly. Then the DVD continues and the speaker finishes the phrase.

It will take approximately four minutes to do the exercise. After completing the exercise answer the study questions and do the follow-up. Turn on the DVD player and find this selection. Take time to look at the title and the speaker's face before proceeding with the exercise. Think about what possible ideas may be presented by this speaker in relation to this topic. You can complete this exercise in one of two ways. Preferably, you will record your spoken answers by using a video camera or a tape recorder. To do this, find this selection on the DVD and prepare your recording device to record your answers. Turn on your recording device first and then turn on the DVD player.

As soon as you hear the beep tone you should complete the idea in spoken English. After the beep and a brief pause, the speaker completes the thought. Speak loudly enough for your recorder to pick up both the speaker's voice and your voice.

If you realize a few seconds later that another ending would make better sense there, say that ending and keep listening to the message and for the next beep. This process of inserting a more appropriate word is the process of self-correction or repair. You will record both of your answers. During this exercise it is important to cut off the "inner critic," or the tendency to criticize yourself either silently or out loud. You will distract yourself and lose precious time if you criticize yourself instead of concentrating on the message.

The second and less preferred way to respond to the exercise is as follows: if you are not working in an environment that will allow you to say your answers out loud, then you can listen to the speaker and write your answers, as soon as you hear the beep, in the space provided in the transcript.

Study Questions

1. Listen to your recording of your voice while reading the transcript. Write your answers from the recording in the space provided in the transcript.

2. Compare your answers with the words that were deleted from the transcript. The words deleted from the transcript are listed at the end of the transcript. For each phrase that you completed, state how you decided what kind of information would logically fit in the blank.

____

____

____

____

____

3. Circle any answers that do not make sense. Put a double underline under your answers that do make sense. Replace any circled words with words that do make sense in this context. Write those replacement words here and number them according to the blanks the words fill.

4. Write at least one alternate answer that makes sense for each blank in the transcript.

5. If any of the utterances that you recorded were comments to yourself about your work, write them down and state the effect of these comments on the message. If you video recorded your work, check the recording to see if your nonverbal behaviors added to or detracted from the message. Look for facial expressions, body movements, or hand movements that could affect the message.

____

____

____

____

Transcript for *My Favorite Teacher,* Maureen Lewnes

Hello. My name is Maureen Lewnes. I'd like to share with you, uh, my favorite teacher from elementary school. I know many of us have had, uh, fond memories of school, and certain people at, uh, those times of our life stand out. Um, my third grade teacher (her name was Miss Fenton) and she was very special to me. Um, I think when I first had her in third grade is when I decided myself *1.* ______________________________, which was a very early age to, uh, decide upon a career. Um, I was very blessed because when I got to sixth grade, 2. ______________________________, who happened to be Mrs. Fenton under her married name, so I was enabled to have my favorite teacher two years in a row.

Um, as life progressed, um, I became a teacher. Um, stopped teaching and raised my own family and went back to teaching. One evening I was reviewing, uh, a videotape for some lessons. Um, the videotape had been, uh, borrowed from a colleague of mine. And I'm sitting at home, uh, reviewing the art lessons on this video and 11:00 at night on a Sunday evening, who should appear on the television screen 3. ______________________________, Miss Fenton, or Mrs. Hugh. Um, she had retired and had developed an art series on video. What was wonderful about this is, I—through the video, um, company 4. ______________________________. Um, not only was I able to share my teach—uh, previous teaching experience with my students, 5. ______________________________. And sh—um, she shared some of her teaching techniques, uh, with my fellow colleagues. It was a wonderful, uh, reintroduction of my favorite teacher into my life and, um, I realized that some of the things that I say to my students 6. ______________________________.

Answer Key

1. *to become a teacher*
2. *I had Mrs. Hugh*
3. *but my old favorite teacher*
4. *I was able to track her down*
5. *but I was able to bring her to my classroom*
6. *are direct quotes from my favorite teacher*

Five-Step Follow-up

Step 1 Observation

Review your answers to the study questions.

Step 2 Selection

Refer to your answer to Study Question 3. The circled words are those that do not make sense in this context.

Step 3 Analysis

For each circled response, state why it does not make sense. State why you chose the response you did. Refer to your answer to Study Question 4 and state why your alternate answer is a more acceptable answer.

____

____

___

___

Step 4

Assessment

What effect did errors have on the meaning of the overall message? Evaluate the effect of the errors in terms of "serious" or "not serious." A serious error means that the original meaning of the message was lost. A nonserious error may change the meaning slightly, but the meaning would still be understood in generally the same way as the meaning of the original message.

___

___

___

___

Step 5

Action

Develop a plan for action based on your analysis and assessment. Once you have determined the effect of word choices on the meaning of the message, you can work to develop rapid and accurate phrase-level pattern inference skills. One way to develop this skill with written material is to work with a friend who can read from a magazine or book and omit the endings of sentences. The reader should mark the phrases that are omitted. Use a tape recorder to record your work and check it for accuracy by comparing your recording with the printed material that was used. You can use the study questions and follow-up to check your work.

___

___

___

___

EXERCISE 8.2

Volunteering

AMY BOUCK

Directions

In this two minute exercise, the speaker is interrupted with a beep tone. When you hear the beep it means you should complete the phrase. Enough time is provided on the DVD for you to provide your answer if you answer promptly. Then the DVD continues and the speaker finishes the phrase.

It will take approximately four minutes to do the exercise. After completing the exercise answer the study questions and do the follow-up. Turn on the DVD player and find this selection. Take time to look at the title and the speaker's face before proceeding with the exercise. Think about what possible ideas may be presented by this speaker in relation to this topic. You can complete this exercise in either of two ways. Preferably, you will record your spoken answers by using a video camera or a tape recorder. To do this, find this selection on the DVD and prepare your recording device to record your answers. Turn on your recording device first and then turn on the DVD player.

As soon as you hear the beep tone you should complete the idea in spoken English. After the beep and a brief pause, the speaker completes the thought. Speak loudly enough so that your recorder will pick up both the speaker's voice and your voice.

If you realize a few seconds later that another ending would make better sense there, say that ending and keep listening to the message and for the next beep. This process of inserting a more appropriate word is the process of self-correction. You will record both of your answers. During this exercise it is important to cut off the "inner critic," or the tendency to criticize yourself either silently or out loud. You will distract yourself and lose precious time if you criticize yourself instead of concentrating on the message.

The second and less preferred way to respond to the exercise is as follows: if you are not working in an environment that will allow you to say your answers out loud, then you can listen to the speaker and write your answers, as soon as you hear the beep, in the space provided in the transcript.

Study Questions

1. Listen to your recording of your voice while reading the transcript. Write your answers from the recording in the space provided in the transcript.

2. Compare your answers with the words that were deleted from the transcript. The words deleted from the transcript are listed at the end of the transcript. For each phrase that you completed, state how you decided what kind of information would logically fit in the blank.

   ____

   ____

   ____

   ____

3. Circle any answers that do not make sense. Put a double underline under your answers that do make sense. Replace any circled words with words that do make sense in this context. Write those replacement words here and number them according to the blanks the words fill.

   ____

   ____

   ____

   ____

4. Write at least one alternate phrase that makes sense for each of your answers. Check a thesaurus or dictionary to be sure that the words you are using mean what you think they mean and that the meaning is relevant to this context.

   ____

   ____

   ____

   ____

5. If any of the utterances that you recorded were comments to yourself about your work, write them down and state the effect of these comments on the message. If you video recorded your work, check the recording to see if your nonverbal behaviors added to or detracted from the message. Look for facial expressions, body movements, or hand movements that could affect the message.

Transcript for *Volunteering,* Amy Bouck

Hi. My name is Amy Bouck and I'm going to tell you about my position as a volunteer at the hospital. I got this position through the Health Sciences department at my university. They were raffling off these positions, and I was assigned to the emergency room at the hospital.

In the emergency room my duties include changing the beds (or gurneys); um, chaperoning male physicians while they treat, uh, female patients; uh, going down to the basement to the linens department to get new linens for the area; uh, rushing samp—blood samples to the lab; or transporting patients from one area to another, such as from their beds to radiology to get x-rays done, or from their beds to, uh, their rooms if they get admitted.

There are three areas in the emergency room. Area one is for the very seriously injured. These include *1.* ______________________ ____. Uh, and area two is exclusively for children. Only pedia— pediatricians 2. ________________________________. In area three is the, uh, least critically injured patients. These include 3. ____ ____ — things like that. Also in the emergency room there's an emergency radiology department and the emergency lab where *4.* ________ ______________________.

Uh, one of my favorite parts about working in the hospital is being able to observe *5.* __________________________ ________. Uh, we have these rooms called the resuscitation rooms where people who are very seriously injured 6. ______________ ______________________ get, uh, get taken in to be worked on if they can't make it all the way up to the operating room. Uh, also I like to go help in radiology and in this you help patients stay in one place so they can get a *7.* ______________________.

Uh, working at the hospital has been probably one of my favorite experiences and I *8.* ______________________________ ________.

Answer Key

1. *cardiac arrests, gunshot wounds, stabbing, and uh, sometimes seizures*
2. *work there to treat the children*
3. *ones with shortness of breath, minor leg breaks or arm breaks, um, stomach cramps and food poisoning—*
4. *where they read bloo—blood samples*
5. *all the procedures that go on*
6. *need immediate treatment*

7. *steady shot, or x-ray*
8. *hope to continue to do so*

Five-Step Follow-up

Step 1 Observation

Review your answers to the study questions.

Step 2 Selection

Refer to your answer to Study Question 3. The circled words are those that do not make sense in this context.

Step 3 Analysis

For each circled response, state why it does not make sense. State why you chose the response you did. Refer to your answer to Study Question 4 and state why your alternate answer is a more acceptable answer.

____

____

____

____

Step 4 Assessment

What effect did errors have on the meaning of the overall message? Evaluate the effect of the errors in terms of "serious" or "not serious." A serious error means that the original meaning of the message was lost. A nonserious error may change the meaning slightly, but the meaning would still be understood in generally the same way as the original message.

____

____

____

____

Step 5 **Action**

Develop a plan for action based on your analysis and assessment. Once you have determined the effect of word choices on the meaning of the message, you can work to develop rapid and accurate phrase-level pattern inference skills. One way to develop this skill with written material is to work with a friend who can read from a magazine or book and omit the endings of sentences. The reader should mark the phrases that are omitted. Use a tape recorder to record your work and check it for accuracy by comparing your recording with the printed material that was used. You can use the study questions and follow-up to check your work.

____

____

____

____

EXERCISE 8.3

How to Trace Your Family Tree

MAUREEN LEWNES

Directions

In this two minute exercise, the speaker is interrupted with a beep tone. When you hear the beep it means you should complete the phrase. Enough time is provided on the DVD for you to provide your answer if you answer promptly. Then the DVD continues and the speaker finishes the phrase.

It will take approximately thirteen minutes to do the exercise. After completing the exercise answer the study questions and do the follow-up. Turn on the DVD player and find this selection. Take time to look at the title and the speaker's face before proceeding with the exercise. Think about what possible ideas may be presented by this speaker in relation to this topic. You can complete this exercise in either of two ways. Preferably, you will record your spoken answers by using a video camera or a tape recorder. To do this, find this selection on the DVD and prepare your recording device to record your answers. Turn on your recording device first and then turn on the DVD player.

As soon as you hear the beep tone you should complete the idea in spoken English. After the beep and a brief pause, the speaker completes the thought. Speak loudly enough for your recorder to pick up both the speaker's voice and your voice.

If you realize a few seconds later that another ending would make better sense there, say that ending and keep listening to the message and for the next beep. This process of inserting a more appropriate word is the process of self-correction. You will record both of your answers. During this exercise it is important to cut off the "inner critic," or the tendency to criticize yourself either silently or out loud. You will distract yourself and lose precious time if you criticize yourself instead of concentrating on the message.

The second and less preferred way to respond to the exercise is as follows: if you are not working in an environment that will allow you to say your answers out loud, then you can listen to the speaker and write your answers, as soon as you hear the beep, in the space provided in the transcript.

Study Questions

1. Listen to your recording of your voice while reading the transcript. Write your answers from the recording in the space provided in the transcript.

2. Compare your answers with the words that were deleted from the transcript. The words deleted from the transcript are listed at the end of the transcript. For each phrase that you completed, state how you decided what kind of information would logically fit in the blank.

___

___

___

___

3. Circle any answers that do not make sense. Put a double underline under your answers that do make sense. Replace any circled words with words that do make sense in this context. Write those replacement words here and number them according to the blanks they fill.

___

___

4. Write at least one alternate ending that makes sense for ten of your answers. Check a thesaurus or dictionary to be sure that the words you are using mean what you think they mean and that the meaning is relevant to this context.

5. If any of the utterances that you recorded were comments to yourself about your work, write them down and state the effect of these comments on the message. If you video recorded your work, check the recording to see if your nonverbal behaviors added to or detracted from the message. Look for facial expressions, body movements, or hand movements that could affect the message.

Transcript for *How to Trace Your Family Tree*, Maureen Lewnes

Hello. My name is Maureen Lewnes and today I'm going to share with you my hobby, which also happens to be the fastest-growing hobby in the United States. My hobby is genealogy: the study of *1.* ______________________________. Uh, this hobby is popular not only in the United States, but around the world, as people search for their roots. Uh, one of the first things that you need to do if you are interested in finding out about your family is to gather as much family history as you can from *2.* ______________________________ ______________. Search out your relatives and find out what they know. It's helpful to tape record or videotape, uh, interviews if you have the opportunity, but letters *3.* ______________________________ __________. An initial, uh, form letting your relatives know that you are, uh, searching out your family history and gathering information from them often, uh, is a great way to crack open the door and *4.* ______________________________.

From those family histories you will able to get some leads to start *5.* ______________________________. There are many places in the United States that you can go for additional resources after you have *6.* ______________________________. One of the first things you need to do is look at a map and find out not only where the city is th—that perhaps your ancestor was born, but *7.* ____ ________________. You must find out the county name. Now there's some guides that will *8.* ______________________________ ______________. One of the best books, um, that is the bible of most genealogists is called The Handy Book. And this is, uh, produced and published by Everton Publi—Publishers in Utah. Um, The Handy Book, uh, lets you know what county records are available, whether it's birth, *9.* ______________________________ ____________________. It lets you know whether a county name has changed. Perhaps, um, your ancestor was born in Green County in 1880 but in 1879 that county originally was Orange County. You would need to know about that change if you were trying to *10.* ______________________________ ____________________. They would not be found under Green County, *11.* ______________________________.

Um, beyond maps and The Handy Book there are other books that are, uh, very important basic *12.* ____________________ ____________________. You would need, um, The Red Book, which is by Ancestry Publishers or a book called The Source. They also have, um, basic maps and, *13.* ____________________. They tell you where the county seats are located and how you can contact them, including phone numbers, uh, for additional information on how to *14.* ____________________ ____________________. Now, we go beyond in government information to um, states wh—where great archives have, um, co—compilations of materials available to you, many of them *15.* ____________________. Um, you also have the federal government National Archives, which can help you. Both state sources and federal sources, um, have censuses on the states. And those censuses list *16.* ____________________ ____________________. Um, you're very, uh, easily, uh, guided to those resources through indexes and a numbering system and a soundex code which, um, gives each letter a sound, um, tabulation to make it easy for you to research *17.* ____________________ ____________________. In addition, the federal sources have military and pension records. If you go back to the county seat you can also, if you can't find your pr—uh, ancestor on the censuses you can look over *18.* ______________________________. And oftentimes there might be other records, um, for welfare for the poor, or, um, passenger *19.* ______________________ that are available to you.

Outside of government resources there are many historical societies, both at the state *20.* ______________________ ______________. And also there are larger historical societies that are regional, such as the New England Genealogical His—and Historical Society. Or you might want to go, uh, and research in Virginia at the National Genealogical Society. They give you a great deal, uh, number of pointers and, um, they also—most of these, uh, historical societies publish quarterly newsletters which give you new hints, offer, uh, query columns where you *21.* ______________ ______________________________________.

Of course, with the advent of technology we have a lot *22.* ______________________________________ ______________. Um, with computers we now have CD-ROM and on that CD-ROM there are phone, uh, number listings, uh, by family name so you might be able to trace your family, uh, through, uh, if you have the same *23.* ______________________ in a particular town you might be able to get leads that way. Also there are many vital statistics that have been recorded on CD- ROM. Or perhaps you want to get on the Internet. Or use an on-line service in a chat group where you can ma—uh, make ties with other *24.* ______________________________________ ______________. And I've found that with my hobby I've met many wonderful people across this country and outside this country who've *25.* ______________________________________. And when you find someone with the last surname that you share it's really 26. ____. Of course, everyone has that one or two skeletons in the closet. I personally find it more interesting and exciting, and many times, um, uh, informative of the history of a particular country, uh, when I, um, do research and do 27. ______________________________________. For example, uh, I have a third great-grandfather and there had been a rumor in—in our family that he had died in jail. My husband and I traveled to Canada. We went to, um, Brockville, Ontario and uh, we were able to trace from a newspaper article and found that my grandfather indeed had 28. ____________________________________. And she had, uh, put him in jail because he was a bigamist. She had 12 children at the time, with the youngest being one year old. Uh, however, this brave lady locked him up because he had 29. ____________________________________. Now, when you put that in historical context it becomes more interesting when you know that at that particular time in the 1860s in Canada that di—divorce was not, 30. ______________________________. And so, uh, people took options that, 31. ____. As I traced along I fou—I guessed that my, uh, grandfather was put into a nearby prison and the next town over was Kingston, Ontario. And in Kingston, at the federal penitentiary, um, across the street was 32. __________________________. So my husband and I went over there, had a very nice tour of the archive and went through 33. ______________________________. From the newspaper article we were able to trace, um, that indeed, 34. ____. As we went through, uh, the prison records it was interesting because at that period of time in that culture, uh, they, part of the punishment for the prisoner was

35. ______________________________. Anytime a prisoner broke that silence, *36.*______________________________ ______________________________. So, after 130 years I had my grandfather's—my great-great-grandfather's words. And what I came to find out was that he was very ill when he went into prison and he *37.* ______________________________. And, uh, his words were words of complaint about cold and *38.* ______________________________. Um, so that was *39.* ______________________________. Many people might want to hide that fact, but for me it—it really made history *40.* ______________________________. It made me understand some of the trials that my grandmother went through and also some of the trials that *41.* ______________________________ ______________________________.

Answer Key

1. *family history*
2. *living members of your family*
3. *work just as well*
4. *let them know what you're up to*
5. *your detective work*
6. *those basic leads from your family*
7. *where that city is located within the state*
8. *help you with this*
9. *marriage or death, vital statistics*
10. *ch—uh trace that ancestor's parents*
11. *but Orange County*
12. *tools for the beginning genealogist*
13. *um, statistics*
14. *proceed with your search*
15. *at no charge*
16. *most of your—your ancestors*

17. *your family name*
18. *tax rolls and land records*
19. *lists*
20. *level, and, um, uh, county level*
21. *can put in ads to help find other relatives*
22. *more tools and resources at our fingertips*
23. *surname*
24. *people that are searching your line*
25. *been very helpful*
26. *exciting, and—and you're instant family*
27. *find a skeleton*
28. *been put in jail by my grandmother*
29. *strayed from, um, their household*
30. *um, available to people*
31. *um, we might not take today*
32. *an archive*
33. *the microfilm*
34. *my grandfather had been a prisoner there*
35. *a code of silence*
36. *um, their words were recorded*
37. *died three months later of tuberculosis*
38. *feeling ill*
39. *kind of an interesting, um, situation*
40. *come alive*
41. *my grandfather went through*

Five-Step Follow-up

Step 1 Observation

Review your answers to the study questions.

Step 2 Selection

Refer to your answer to Study Question 3. The circled words are those that do not make sense in this context.

Step 3 Analysis

For each circled response, state why it does not make sense. State why you chose the response you did. Refer to your answer to Study Question 4 and state why your alternate answer is a more acceptable answer.

____

____

____

____

Step 4 Assessment

What effect did errors have on the meaning of the overall message? Evaluate the effect of the errors in terms of "serious" or "not serious." A serious error means that the original meaning of the message was lost. A nonserious error may change the meaning slightly, but the meaning would still be understood in generally the same way as the original message.

____

____

____

____

Step 5 Action

Develop a plan for action based on your analysis and assessment. Once you have determined the effect of word choices on the meaning of the message, you can work to develop rapid and accurate phrase-level pattern inference skills. One way to develop this skill with written material is to work with a friend who can read from a magazine or book and omit the endings of sentences. The reader should mark the phrases that are omitted. Use a tape recorder to record your work and check it for accuracy by comparing your recording with the printed material that was used. You can use the study questions and follow-up to check your work.

____

____

____

____

Progress Tracking Sheet

This sheet is designed to help you keep track of which exercises you have completed and how well you have done on these exercises. See page 12 for a full description of how to use the Progress Tracking Sheet.

Exercise Number	Date	First Performance	Study Questions	Follow-up Activity	Questions and Reminders	Date	Second Performance
Exercise 8.1 Quantitative							
Qualitative							
Exercise 8.2 Quantitative							
Qualitative							
Exercise 8.3 Quantitative							
Qualitative							
Quantitative Totals							

UNIT 9 Multitasking

Introduction

Multitasking means that two or more tasks are performed at the same time. The primary task is generally to listen and repeat. Other tasks that can be performed at the same time as the repetition can include writing or tapping with the hand or foot. In the past, multitasking has been called dual tasking. The term *dual tasking* is a misnomer because cognitive tasks are added to the process of repetition. Repetition is already two tasks at once (listen and repeat). If an additional task such as writing is added, the exercise should be called multitasking. Examples of multitasking include repeating while writing something from memory such as a well-known poem, or writing multiplication tables forward or backward, or even writing numbers as in counting forward or backward. Other tasks that can be added to repetition are motor skills such as finger tapping. When a delay is added to multitasking, it becomes an exercise in developing control over processing time, or decalage.

How well a person manages multitasking events, reveals the ability to divide or shift attention among competing tasks while selecting one for greater focus. Multitasking exercises do not exactly replicate the multitasking that is needed in the interpretation process. Instead, they provide practice on the component parts and provide an opportunity to experience the feeling of managing several tasks at one time while giving greater attention to one over the others. Usually, the main task of listening and repeating is the one that should receive the greater attention. The task that is added to the listen and repeat task is called the distracter task. In general, the performance on the main task is the one we are interested in. The various distracter tasks provide experience in filtering out less important information while continuing to focus on the listen and repeat task. This kind of exercise allows us to know that it is possible to deal with many tasks at the same time. In this unit, three different types of distracter tasks are used. The distracters are graduated in difficulty. The first is writing numbers, the second is tapping with your foot or hand, and the third is writing memorized texts.

The Role of Multitasking in the Interpretation Process

The ability to manage several cognitive tasks at the same time is an essential aspect of the simultaneous interpretation process. Various authors have described the ability to manage several cognitive tasks in relation to the interpretation process. MacWhinney (1997) says that the simultaneous interpreter must have two separate foci of attention at the same time. One focus is on comprehension of the incoming message and the other is on the structure of the output or production. The interpreter's focus on production always occurs after the focus of concentration. Gile (1995) describes the simultaneous interpreting process as a divided-attention task. By this he means that the interpreter must pay attention to several aspects of the process at the same time.

The entire simultaneous interpretation process is heavily dependent on cognitive processing skills. But more than that, these skills must operate on several different levels at the same time. For example, while you are listening and comprehending, you must also transfer the message and, at the same time, find expression for the message in the TL. The expression given to the TL message must also be monitored for sense and corrected if necessary. This is a very brief and simple description of the many processes that occur simultaneously during the interpretation process. Managing so many different cognitive and linguistic tasks all at once is not an automatic or innate process for anyone. Moreover, the multitasking aspect of the process is the most cognitively demanding. Because it is so demanding and may be new for you, you will be using materials found earlier in the video. You will be using materials that are slightly familiar in order to introduce you to this complex process and provide you with a feeling of accomplishment.

After you have completed the three exercises in this unit, you may want to apply these exercise types to other portions of the DVD or to other prerecorded spoken English materials. Use the selections from Unit 4 for the exercises in this unit.

Multitasking Exercises

EXERCISE 9.1

Introduction

DAVID BURNIGHT

For Unit 9 exercises you will use video clips from Unit 4. Select Exercise 4.1 *Introduction* on your DVD.

Directions

In this exercise you will be doing several things at once in order to increase your cognitive processing capacity. It will take approximately one minute to do this exercise. After completing the exercise answer the questions and do the follow-up. Turn on the DVD player and find this selection. You will record your spoken answers. To do this, find this selection on the DVD and prepare your recording device to record your answers.

The primary task is repetition (listen and repeat) and the distracter task is to tap your left foot if you are right-handed or your right foot if you are left-handed in a regular beat while listening. When the selection starts, begin immediate repetition as the primary task and at the same time begin tapping your foot. Turn on your recording device first and then turn on the DVD player and begin repeating while tapping your foot.

Study Questions

1. Listen to the recording of your work and read the transcript. Do your repetitions match the original message? Does your intonation match the speaker's? Does your volume remain audible? Circle the places on the transcript where any of these problems show up. Write down the number of instances of each type of error.

Match message? ____________________

____

____

Intonation? ____________________

Audible?

2. How did the distracter task affect your ability to repeat?

3. Did your ability to repeat vary as you worked thorough the exercise? Examine your performance to see at what points your repetitions were not as good and how you regained your concentration. Explain.

4. How much attention did you need to give to the distracter task? Explain.

5. Repeat this exercise, but this time while repeating tap the hand that you do not use for writing. Tap on the surface in front of you in a steady rhythm. Use the same video passage.

Transcript for *Introduction,* David Burnight

My name is David Burnight. I have been a campus minister at San Diego State University for many years, now retired. I grew up in southern California. I've been a carpenter, a Navy officer, but most of my life I spent being a university pastor on the university campus.

Five-Step Follow-up

Step 1 Observation

Review your answers to the study questions.

Step 2 Selection

Refer to your answer to Study Question 1. The portions of the transcript that you have circled indicate places where the distracter task may have interfered with your repetition process.

Step 3 Analysis

In the areas that you selected in step 2 that indicate errors, analyze those answers more closely. Reflect on your multitasking process at that point and try to determine what caused the breakdown in the repetition process. Write your insights into the process here.

____

____

____

____

Step 4 Assessment

What effect did errors in repetition have on the meaning of the overall message? Evaluate the effect of the errors in terms of "serious" or "not serious." A serious error means that the original meaning of the message was lost. A non-serious error may change the meaning slightly, but the meaning would still be understood in generally the same way as the original message. Did your ability to cope with the distracter task improve as you worked through the selection? Explain your strategies.

____

____

____

Step 5 Action

Develop a plan for action based on your analysis and assessment. For example, if you found that your ability to handle the distracters improved as you worked through the speech, practice it again, either on this video selection or on another one, and see if you can bring your coping strategies into effect sooner in the speech. Be aware of how much attention you are giving to each part of the multitasking exercise.

____

____

____

____

EXERCISE 9.2

The Scare

JEFF HARDISON

Find Exercise 4.2 *The Scare* on your DVD.

Directions

In this exercise you will be doing several things at once in order to increase your cognitive processing capacity. It will take approximately two and a half minutes to do this exercise. After completing the exercise answer the questions and do the follow-up. Turn on the DVD player and find this selection. You will record your spoken answers. To do this, find this selection on the DVD and prepare your recording device to record your answers.

The primary task is repetition (listen and repeat) and the distracter task is to write the Pledge of Allegiance while listening and repeating. Continue writing the Pledge of Allegiance as long as the selection continues. When the selection starts, begin immediate repetition as the primary task and at the same time begin writing. Turn on your recording device first and then turn on the DVD player and begin repeating while writing.

Study Questions

1. Listen to the recording of your work and read the transcript. Do your repetitions match the original message? Does your intonation match the speaker's? Does your volume remain audible? Circle the places on the transcript where any of these problems show up. Write down the number of instances of each type of error.

Match message? ____

Intonation? ____

Audible? ______________________________

____

2. How did the distracter task affect your ability to repeat?

____

____

____

____

3. Did your ability to repeat vary as you worked through the exercise? Examine your performance to see at what points your repetitions were not as good and how you regained your concentration. Explain.

____

____

____

____

4. How much attention did you need to give to the distracter task? Explain.

____

____

____

____

5. Repeat this exercise, but this time write another memorized poem, nursery rhyme, or prayer while repeating. Use the same video passage.

____

Transcript for *The Scare*, Jeff Hardison

Hi. My name is Jeff Hardison and I though I'd talk a little bit about some of the interesting times I had growing up in the family that I did. Real briefly, my family came from Cuba and so I spent a lot of my time growing up in the household of my grandparents and that's how I ended growing up as Cuban as I did.

Um, my grandparents' daughter, their youngest daughter my aunt Griselle and I used to hang out a lot together. But I was kind of like the little brother who always was tagging along and she would get annoyed with that. But she found interesting ways to remind me that sometimes I might not want to do that. And there was this one time I can remember that she was going to stay up late with some friends of hers to watch a horror movie. And ah, this particular horror movie was a werewolf movie. And I just pleaded and pleaded until finally she gave in and let me watch it with her and her friends; she was having a sleepover at the time. Well, when the movie was over, I went, ah went to sleep. And of course, you know, I was a little kid at the time, I wasn't much older than eight. And, ah so I fell asleep. I was probably a bit scared at the time. Well my aunt had this big bear, teddy bear that her boyfriend had won for her in a carnival. It must have been about yay big; I would say maybe four feet, four and half feet. And what she did is she waited until I was good and asleep and then got the bear, put it nose to nose with me and then woke me up.

Well, of course I screamed bloody murder. Um about this time my grandmother came running in. And you have to picture, my grandmother is about four feet tall. She was just a tiny little woman. And she was so mad at my aunt, she like pulled off her sandals and started chasing her around the house. It was the funniest thing I'd ever seen. Actually, it was almost worth it to see that last piece happen.

Five-Step Follow-up

Step 1 Observation

Review your answers to the study questions.

Step 2 Selection

Refer to your answer to Study Question 1. The portions of the transcript that you have circled indicate places where the distracter task may have interfered with your repetition process.

Step 3 Analysis

In the areas that you selected in step 2 that indicate errors, analyze those answers more closely. Reflect on your multitasking process at that point and try to determine what caused the breakdown in the repetition process. Write your insights into the process here.

Step 4 Assessment

What effect did errors in repetition have on the meaning of the overall message? Evaluate the effect of the errors in terms of "serious" or "not serious." A serious error means that the original meaning of the message was lost. A non-serious error may change the meaning slightly, but the meaning would still be understood in generally the same way as the original message. Did your ability to cope with the distracter task improve as you worked through the selection? Explain your strategies.

____

____

____

____

Step 5

Action

Develop a plan for action based on your analysis and assessment. For example, if you found that your ability to handle the distracters improved as you worked through the speech, practice it again, either on this video selection or another one, and see if you can bring your coping strategies into effect sooner in the speech. Be aware of how much attention you are giving to each part of the multitasking exercise.

____

____

____

____

EXERCISE 9.3

The Cake

PAM CRISOSTOMO

Find Exercise 4.3 *The Cake* on your DVD.

Directions

In this exercise you will be doing several things at once in order to increase your cognitive processing capacity. It will take approximately five minutes to do this exercise. After completing the exercise answer the questions. Turn on the DVD player and find this selection. You will record your spoken answers. To do this, find this selection on the DVD and prepare your recording device to record your answers.

The primary task is repetition (listen and repeat) and the distracter task is to write numbers while listening and repeating. When the selection starts, begin immediate repetition as the primary task and at the same time begin writing the numbers from 2 to 100, counting forward by twos. Turn on your recording device first and then turn on the DVD player and begin writing numbers.

Study Questions

1. Listen to the recording of your work and read the transcript. Do your repetitions match the original message? Does your intonation match the speaker's? Does your volume remain audible? Circle the places on the transcript where problems in any of these areas occur. Write down the number of instances of each type of error.

Match message? ______________________________

____

____

Intonation? ______________________________

____

____

Audible? ______________________________

____

2. Look at the numbers that you wrote. Were you able to maintain an accurate counting pattern? If you were, then the distracter task did not interfere very much and you were able to manage all three tasks of listening, repeating, and writing at the same time.

____

____

____

____

3. How did the counting task affect your ability to repeat?

4. Did your ability to repeat vary as you worked through the exercise? Examine your performance to see at what points your repetitions were not as good and how you regained your concentration. Explain.

5. Do this exercise again, but this time write the numbers from 1 to 100 by counting forward by threes. Compare the results of the two exercises. You can do the exercise again and count backward by ones. You can use the same video selection or any other selection on the DVD except those in the number repetition unit.

Transcript for *The Cake*, Pam Crisostomo

My name is Pam Crisostomo and I'm going to share a personal experience that I've had. I'm the oldest of four children and I'm 19 years old. And I have a sister whose name is Phyllis and she's 13 and my sister's—next sister's name is Patty, and she's 12 and I have a little brother whose name is Noel and he's 8, and so there's ten and a half years between me and Noel. Um, I was an only child for a very long time, and I was supposed to be an only child until I remember one Christmas where I asked my mother, um, well I told my mother that instead of asking Santa for toys this Christmas, I wanted a baby sister instead. So a couple of months later I had a baby sister; her name was Phyllis and so she was born in April. And in June of 1984 we were preparing for a big baptismal party for Phyllis and she was gonna get baptized at St. Charles Church; and we were gonna have a lot of visitors over—probably about, I dunno maybe over, about maybe 300 visitors. And in the process my mom had a friend whose husband made cakes. And so my mom's friend's husband made a cake that was, um, about 20 x 30—so it was a huge cake, it was decorated really nicely and there was a stork on it and there was a baby—baby in the stork—in the stork's beak, and I just remember how great a cake it was. And so my mom, um, wanted to hide the cake so like the visitors who were going to spend the night, um, coming later that evening wouldn't see the cake—kind of so she would keep it as a surprise for everybody else. And so she and her friend put the cake in a big box and then we put it in our study. Um, so later that evening my sister Phyllis' godmother came and along with her godmother she brought her husband and her two girls. And I was excited because, I mean I was pretty much a very lonely child and so having playmates was like a big deal for me and I was really excited that I had a new sister named Phyllis who was born. And so one of the girls, her name was Lisa and she was my age and her sister Rena, um, was younger—was a year younger than both of—both of us.

So we decided that we'd play a game of hide and seek. So we were playing hide and seek and we were laughing, we were having fun, I mean as all little kids do, and at one point Lisa was "it" and Rena and I hid—hid, like in the living room and we were found very easily, and so I guess after 3 or 4 rounds Lisa—it was Lisa's turn to be "it" and so Lisa was "it". And it just wasn't working right; we were having fun, we were having a lot of fun but people were finding each other too easily. So I took Lisa—Lisa and I hid in the study room 'cause I figured that would be the best place to hide. And so Lisa and I went to the study and we ran really quickly and I remember the door slamming really loud and it was a wonder that Rena didn't find us just by the sound of the door slamming. And so we were really tired. I remember, like, laughing really hard. And Lisa decided to sit down. And Lisa sat down on the box that had the cake in it. And it was horrendous. Um, I screamed 'cause the box that she had sat on had the cake in it and so part of the cake was ruined. So I screamed and I called my mom and all I remember was I got spanked. I was six years old and I got spanked, whereas Lisa and Rena didn't get in trouble at all, but, um, my mom said that it was my fault because this was my house and we weren't supposed to be in the study anyway. And the cake was ruined—this big, beautiful cake was ruined.

So, I kinda thought, when I was, y'know, little I thought that was kind of an injustice for me because it wasn't my fault. All I did was go and play hide and seek and I remember my dad telling the visitors the next day when the cake was out, um, about how the kids were playing and that's why half of the cake was ruined. But that's something I'm never gonna forget, kind of like one of my injustices. But I look back now and I laugh, and I'm sure my mom laughs too.

Five-Step Follow-up

Step 1 Observation

Review your answers to the study questions.

Step 2 Selection

Refer to your answer to Study Question 1. The portions of the transcript that you have circled indicate places where the distracter task may have interfered with your repetition process

Step 3 Analysis

In the areas that you selected in step 2 that indicate errors, analyze those answers more closely. Reflect on your multitasking process at that point and try to determine what caused the breakdown in the repetition process. Write your insights into the process here.

____

____

____

____

Step 4 Assessment

What effect did errors in repetition have on the meaning of the overall message? Evaluate the effect of the errors in terms of "serious" or "not serious." A serious error means that the original meaning of the message was lost. A non-serious error may change the meaning slightly, but the meaning would still be understood in generally the same way as the original message. Did your ability to cope with the distracter task improve as you worked through the selection? Explain your strategies.

____

____

____

____

Step 5 Action

Develop a plan for action based on your analysis and assessment. For example, if you found that your ability to handle the distracters improved as you worked through the speech, practice it again, either on this video selection or another one, and see if you can bring your coping strategies into effect sooner in the speech. Be aware of how much attention you are giving to each part of the multitasking exercise.

____

____

____

____

Progress Tracking Sheet

This sheet is designed to help you keep track of which exercises you have completed and how well you have done on these exercises. See page 12 for a full description of how to use the Progress Tracking Sheet.

Exercise Number	Date	First Performance	Study Questions	Follow-up Activity	Questions and Reminders	Date	Second Performance
Exercise 9.1 Quantitative							
Qualitative							
Exercise 9.2 Quantitative							
Qualitative							
Exercise 9.3 Quantitative							
Qualitative							
Quantitative Totals							

References

The American Heritage Dictionary of the English Language, 3rd Edition (1992). Houghton-Mifflin.

Anderson, G., & Stauffer, L. (1990). *Identifying standards for the training of interpreters for deaf people.* University of Arkansas. Rehabilitation Research and Training Center on Deafness and Hearing Impairment.

Atkinson, R.C., & Shiffrin, R.M. (1968). Human memory: A proposed system and its control processes. In K.W. Spence (Ed.), *The Psychology of learning and motivation: Advances in research and theory.* New York: Academic Press.

Baddeley, A. (1990). *Human memory: Theory and practice.* Hillsdale, NJ: Erlbaum.

Bowen, D., & Bowen, M. (1989). Aptitude for interpreting. In L. Gran & J. Dodds (Eds.), *The theoretical and practical aspects of teaching conference interpretation* (pp. 109–127). Trieste, Italy: Campanotto Editore, Udine.

Bruner, J. S. (1966). *The process of education.* Cambridge, MA: Harvard University Press.

Cokely, D. (1986). The effects of time lag on interpreter errors. *Sign Language Studies.* 53. 341–376.

Cokely, D. (1992a). The effect of lag time on interpreter errors. In D. Cokely (Ed.), *Sign language interpreters and interpreting* (pp.39–69). Silver Spring, MD: Linstok Press.

Cokely, D. (1992b). *Interpretation:A sociolinguistic model.* Silver Spring, MD: Linstok Press.

Conference of Interpreter Trainers (1998). *CIT position paper: Instructional class siz- interpreter training,* 18 (3), p.21.

Dancette, J. (1997). Mapping meaning and comprehension in translation. In J. Danks, et al. (Eds.), *Cognitive processes in translation and interpreting* (pp. 77–104). Thousand Oaks, CA: Sage Publications.

Danks, J. et al. (Eds.) (1997). *Cognitive processes in translation and interpreting.* Thousand Oaks, CA: Sage Publications.

DeGroot, A. (1997). The cognitive study of translation and interpretation. In J. Danks, et al. (Eds.), *Cognitive processes in translation and interpreting* (pp.25–57). Thousand Oaks, CA: Sage Publications.

Fleetwood, E. (1998). Personal communication.

Funk and Wagnall's Standard Dictionary (1983). New York: Harper Collins.

Gile, D. (1995). *Basic concepts and models for interpreter and translator training.* Philadelphia: John Benjamins.

Gile, D. (1997). Conference interpreting as a cognitive management problem. In J. Danks, et al. (Eds.), *Cognitive processes in translation and interpreting* (pp.196–215). Thousand Oaks, CA: Sage Publications.

Gonzalez, R. et al. (1991). *Fundamentals in court interpretation: Theory, policy and practice.* Durham, NC: Carolina Academic Press.

Ingram, R., (1984). Teaching declage skills. In M. L. McIntire (Ed.), *New dialogues in interpreter education: Proceedings of the Fourth National Conference of Interpreter Trainers Convention* (pp. 291–308). Silver Spring: MD.

Johnson, R.E., Patrie, C., & Roy, C. (1988). *Master of Arts in Interpretation Curriculum* Washington, DC: Gallaudet University.

Kalina, S. (1992). Discourse processing and interpreting strategies-An approach to the teaching of interpreting. In C. Dollerup & A. Loddegaard (Eds.), *Teaching translation and interpreting training, talent and experience* (pp. 251–258). Philadelphia: John Benjamins.

Kelly, L. (1979). *The true interpreter: A history of translation theory and practice in the west.* New York: St. Martin's Press.

Kurz, I. (1992). Shadowing exercises in interpreter training. In C. Dollerup & A. Loddegaard (Eds.), *Teaching translation and interpreting training, talent and experience* (pp. 245–250). Philadelphia: John Benjamins.

Lambert, S. (1992). Aptitude testing for simultaneous interpretation at the University of Ottawa. In L. Gran & J. Dodds (Eds.), *The interpreter's newsletter.* Trieste: University of Trieste Press.

Lambert, S. (1989). Plenary session. In S. Wilcox (Ed.), *New dimensions in interpreter education: Evaluation and critique* (pp. 113–125). Conference of Interpreter Trainers.

Lambert, S. (1988). A human information processing and cognitive approach to the training of simultaneous interpreters. In D. L. Hammond (Ed.), *Language at crossroads: Proceedings of the 29th Annual Conference of the American Translators Association* (pp. 379-387). Medford, NJ: Learned Information.

Larson, M. (1984). *Meaning based translation: A guide to cross-language equivalence.* Lanham, MD: University of America Press.

Longley, P. (1989). The use of aptitude testing in the selection of students for conference interpretation training. In L. Gran & J. Dodds (Eds.), *The theoretical and practical aspects of teaching conference interpretation* (pp. 105–109). Campanotto Editore, Udine.

MacWhinney (1997). Simultaneous interpretation and the competition model. In J. Danks, et al. (Eds.), *Cognitive processes in translation and interpreting* (pp. 215–233). Thousand Oaks, CA: Sage Publications.

Moser, B. (1997). Beyond curiosity: Can interpreting research meet the challenge? In J. Danks, et al. (Eds.), *Cognitive processes in translation and interpreting* (pp. 176-195). Thousand Oaks, CA: Sage Publications.

Moser–Mercer (1983). Defining aptitude for simultaneous interpretation. In M. L. McIntire (Ed.), *New dialogues in interpreter education: Proceedings of the Fourth National Conference of Interpreter Trainers Convention* (pp. 43–70). Silver Spring, MD: RID Publications.

Oller, J. (1988). Making sense in interpreter education programs: Evaluation. In S. Wilcox (Ed.), *New dimensions in interpreter education: Evaluation and critique. Proceedings of the Seventh National Convention of the Conference of Interpreter Trainers.* (pp. 1–20). Conference of Interpreter Trainers.

Roberts, R. (1987). Spoken language interpreting vs. sign language interpreting. In K. Kummer (Ed.), *Proceedings of the 28th Annual Conference of the American Translators Association* (pp. 293–307). Albuquerque, NM: Learned Information Inc.

Roberts, R. (1992). Student competencies: Defining, teaching, and evaluating. In E.A. Winston (Ed.), *Student competencies: Defining, teaching, and evaluating* (pp. 1–18). Conference of Interpreter Trainers.

Schweda Nicholson, N. (1988). Interpreter evaluation: The whole does not always equal the sum of its parts. In S. Wilcox (Ed.), *New dimensions in interpreter education: Evaluation and critique* (pp. 65–68). Conference of Interpreter Trainers.

Schweda Nicholson, N. (1996). Perspectives on the role of memory in interpretation: A critical review of recent literature. In M. Jerome-O'Keefe (Ed.), *Global Vision: Proceedings of the 37th Annual Conference of the American Translators Association* (pp. 99–113). Alexandria, VA: The American Translator's Association.

Seal, B. (1999) Educational interpreters document efforts to improve. *VIEWS,* 16(2), p. 14. Silver Spring, MD: Registry of Interpreters for the Deaf.

Seleskovitch, D., & Lederer, M. (1989). *A systematic approach to teaching interpretation.* Silver Spring, MD: Registry of Interpreters for the Deaf.

Shreve, G., & Koby, G. (1997). Introduction: What's in the black box? Cognitive science and translation studies. In J. Danks, et al. (Eds.), *Cognitive processes in translation and interpreting* (pp. xi–xviii). Thousand Oaks, CA: Sage Publications.

Sunnari, M. (1995). Processing strategies in simultaneous interpreting: Experts vs. novices. In C. Nixon (Ed.), *Connections: Proceedings of the 36th Annual Conference of the American Translators Association* (pp. 157–165). Alexandria, VA: American Translator's Association.

Taylor, C. (1989). Textual memory and the teaching of consecutive interpretation. In L. Gran & J. Dodds (Eds.), *The Theoretical and practical aspects of teaching conference interpretation* (pp. 177–185). Campanotto Editore, Udine.

Tulvig, E. (1983). *Elements of episodic memory.* Oxford: Oxford University Press.

Washington Post (Jan. 8, 1999). Pfiesteria.

Waubonsee Community College (1993). *Interpreter training programs in the U.S. and Canada.* Sugar Grove, IL: Waubonsee Community College Press.

Ur, P. (1991). *Teaching listening comprehension.* Cambridge, UK: Cambridge University Press.